"Rahim Thawer has written an accessible mental health guide that I'm sure many queer and trans men will benefit from. Reading this guide is like going on a journey with a well-traveled friend holding your hand. The exercises draw on cognitive behavioral therapy (CBT), psychodynamic therapy, and Gestalt therapy. The vignettes reflect a diversity with regards to race, sexuality, gender, age, HIV status, and more that I applaud."

—**Vikram Kolmannskog, DrPhilos,**
professor at the Norwegian Gestalt Therapy Institute;
and author of several books, including *The Empty Chair: Tales from Gestalt Therapy*

"Rahim Thawer's book, *The Mental Health Guide for Cis and Trans Queer Guys*, is timely and offers insight into the experiences of cis and trans individuals, and how they can cope with their own emotions and support others. The book is a much-needed guide for personal and educational use; it introduces the reader to key concepts and therapies such as CBT, Gestalt, and psychodynamic therapy."

—**Alfonso Pezzella, MSc, PGCHE, BSc (Hons),**
director of mental health programs
at Middlesex University London, UK; and chair of
the International Sexuality and Social Work group

"Rahim's writing is a gift—relatable, accessible, and deeply and truly empathetic. His voice reflects his boldness and experience as a therapist and leader, offering love and understanding on every page. With his experience empowering gay men's communities in Canada and beyond, Rahim's words carry wisdom and heart. This book is a must-read for anyone seeking connection, authenticity, and true insight."

—**Aaron Purdie**, executive director of HIM
Health Initiative for Men Society based in BC, Canada; and
registered clinical counselor who practices with 2SLGBTQIA+
people

"A comprehensive guide to the specialized mental health needs of GBTQ men written in a sensitive and respectful manner that will appeal to readers seeking support and a mentally healthier existence. With pertinent topic areas that are unique to the lives of GBTQ men—along with numerous examples, easy-to-follow steps, and exercises—this book is relevant to mental health and well-being at any stage of their life process."

—**Nick J. Mulé, PhD**, professor of social work and sexuality studies at York University, therapist in private practice, and founder of Queer Ontario

"As a sex therapist who explores the specifics of societal and developmental insults and trauma endured by GBTQ guys, this self-help guide uniquely expands on these concepts and puts specific and helpful tools and exercises in the hands of clients who need support but haven't been able to access it."

—**Joe Kort, PhD, LMSW**, author of *Side Guys: It's Still Sex Even If You Don't Have Intercourse*

"Rahim Thawer has written an essential and timely book in these difficult homophobic and transphobic times we live in. Thawer draws upon robust knowledge of diverse therapeutic theories and methods to help readers improve their mental health. Crucially, Rahim explains the impact of societal oppression and frames mental health difficulties in this context, which de-pathologizes common struggles of queer people and is affirming of gender, sexuality, and relationship diversity."

—**Silva Neves**, author of *Sexology*

"This book is a much-needed life raft for queer men. Rahim writes with warmth, empathy, and an ability to translate evidence-based therapeutic knowledge into clear insights and practical tools. The book I wish I'd had as a young, queer man."

—**Kent Burgess, BOT, MPH, GAICD, CEO,** CEO of Your Community Health; and LGBTQIA+ health, mental health, and alcohol and drug services leader

The MENTAL HEALTH GUIDE for CIS & TRANS QUEER GUYS

SKILLS TO COPE & THRIVE AS YOUR AUTHENTIC SELF

RAHIM THAWER, MSW, RSW

New Harbinger Publications, Inc.

Publisher's Note

This publication is designed to provide accurate and authoritative information in regard to the subject matter covered. It is sold with the understanding that the publisher is not engaged in rendering psychological, financial, legal, or other professional services. If expert assistance or counseling is needed, the services of a competent professional should be sought.

All case studies in this book are composites. Any resemblance to persons living or dead is unintentional and entirely coincidental.

NEW HARBINGER PUBLICATIONS is a registered trademark of New Harbinger Publications, Inc.

New Harbinger Publications is an employee-owned company.

Copyright © 2025 by Rahim Thawer
New Harbinger Publications, Inc.
5720 Shattuck Avenue
Oakland, CA 94609
www.newharbinger.com

All Rights Reserved

Cover design by Amy Shoup

Acquired by Georgia Kolias

Edited by M. C. Calvi

Library of Congress Cataloging-in-Publication Data on file

Printed in the United States of America

27   26   25

10   9   8   7   6   5   4   3   2   1   First Printing

CONTENTS

Foreword — v
Introduction — 7

PART 1: YOUR SOCIAL CONTEXT

CHAPTER 1	Coming Out	19
CHAPTER 2	Homophobia, Biphobia, Transphobia	33
CHAPTER 3	Internalized Shame	47
CHAPTER 4	Family and Culture	59
CHAPTER 5	Milestone Hetero-normativity	71
CHAPTER 6	Disenfranchised Grief	81

PART 2: YOUR CONNECTIONS

CHAPTER 7	Seeking Connections	97
CHAPTER 8	Managing Rejection	105
CHAPTER 9	Body-Conscious Culture	117
CHAPTER 10	Endings in Queer Love	127
CHAPTER 11	Boundary Violations	135

PART 3: YOUR HEALTH

CHAPTER 12	Accessing Medical Care	149
CHAPTER 13	Sexual Health	157
CHAPTER 14	Substance Use	167
CHAPTER 15	Aging	181

Conclusion — 187
References — 189

FOREWORD

It's been a long journey to shift our thinking about queerness. Not long ago, and for *generations*, queerness was considered a form of insanity by mental health professionals. It wasn't until 1988 that homosexuality was fully depathologized in the *Diagnostic and Statistical Manual of Mental Disorders* (*DSM*). For transgender folks, it wasn't until 2013. Medical guides like the *DSM* not only established treatments but they also impacted the culture and, most importantly, the way we saw ourselves.

In the 1950s, homosexuality was considered a "sociopathic personality disturbance," equated with alcoholism and criminal behavior. Gender identity was not even in the conversation. In the '60s, homosexuality was downgraded to a "sexual deviation" and attributed to a dysfunctional family, a smothering mother, or a distant father. Terms like "transsexualism" and "gender identity disorder" entered the discourse. In the 1970s, psychiatrists stopped considering homosexuality a disorder. However, transgender folks were still thought of as a problem that required treatment and intervention. And in the 1980s, a new diagnosis emerged: "ego-dystonic homosexuality," which described people who suffered debilitating shame over their gayness, such as a gay man who felt suicidal with guilt over his religion. It was progress, finally acknowledging society's stigma, but it still perpetuated the idea that gayness was the problem, and it justified harmful "cures."

Among the darkest chapters of LGBTQ history are the medieval treatments queer people have endured: electroshock therapy, aversion therapy paired with nausea-inducing drugs, and violent conversion practices. That was for those "lucky" enough to receive professional treatment. For most, the only cures were the closet or jail. By the late 1980s, advocacy and research confirmed that misery over queerness tended to come from the external—stemming from discrimination and societal expectations. Finally, in 1987, "ego-dystonic homosexuality" was removed from the DSM.

Progress has always come with debates. The DSM introduced the concept of "gender dysphoria" in 2013. It reduced stigma and focused on the distress some folks feel about their gender, rather than labeling their identities a disorder. Some argue that including gender dysphoria perpetuates a medicalized view of transgender experiences, while others highlight its importance for accessing affirming healthcare, such as hormone replacement therapy and surgeries, which often require a formal diagnosis.

In the 1980s, a plague of biblical proportions descended on the queer community. AIDS exposed society's refusal to see gay and trans people as human. To many, AIDS was divine retribution and a cosmic joke. Of course, AIDS was not a punishment; it was the result of neglect. But the former idea burrowed itself into the narratives of queer people and spawned shames that have echoed for decades.

For as long as many queers can remember, we have been told we'd never make it to our forties. Sex education, bullies, and movies said we'd die of AIDS, loneliness, or violence. In the '80s and '90s, there were no sitcoms about middle-aged gay men or transitioning trans youth. Maybe a "special episode" about coming out or, of course, HIV. Queers in movies always died; this was by design, and many times mandated by the studios or the law. A gay man's script was written: cast as an angsty, closeted teen, then an addicted, suicidal hustler, then a sexless, fashionable, funny sidekick (under 35), then a white-picket husband or creepy, flaming villain. Then, we'd vanish. If trans folks were in the picture at all, it was either to be made fun of, murdered, be the killers, or all three.

Why would we expect more? So many of our heroes and lovers died by forty. Addiction and suicide rates in our communities are so much higher than those of our straight counterparts. Trans people continue to be in an epidemic of stigma, violence, and financial crisis. Queer people always seem to be in a tug-of-war with the medical field, culture, and politics.

Of course, as of the 2020s, we've also earned rights and built tools and communities unimaginable to our ancestors. We don't need to buy or sell scripts about invisible men or murderous trans women. Guides like the one you are holding are not just new and rare; they are breaking generational suffering. They give us tools to understand our experience on our own terms, not those of a biased or hostile dominant culture. They remind us that what we've sacrificed and valued means the future does not start from scratch. That we get to be the last "first" generation of queer people.

—Leo Herrera
    Artist and activist, director of *The Fathers Project* and author of *Analog Cruising*

INTRODUCTION

Since before you were born, other people have probably had expectations for you and who you were going to be. Those expectations might have been dreams or visions about your future, or hopes or fears for it. The people holding those expectations might have been your parents, grandparents, siblings, extended family, family friends, communities, doctors, or even strangers. The expectations were hopefully good but might have been bad. And perhaps they didn't include you being gay, bisexual, queer, or trans.

Those expectations may not have included you challenging gender norms, loving people of the same gender or multiple genders, or struggling with tensions between your faith or community, and your own authenticity.

It's likely no one expected you to have to deal with the threat (or reality) of homophobia, femmephobia, or transphobia, either. These are all huge obstacles that queer and trans people have to deal with in life—but they're not things we're taught how to handle. Often, the prejudice and hate come from the very people who are supposed to do the teaching.

These problems and threats probably weren't in your own dreams for the future either, back when you were a kid. You may have known early on that you were different, or even that you liked other boys, but I really, truly hope that you didn't have to be aware of or fear things like violence or being disowned. No child should have to deal with violence or rejection, especially for being themselves. But of course, many children do anyway; and you might well have had to deal with these experiences.

The world may have gone through a huge revolution in LGBTQ+ acceptance in the past four decades, but we still have so much further to go. From rejection to homophobia to violence to depression, a lot of really serious issues are more common for gay, bisexual, trans, and queer (GBTQ) guys than for the average person. And dealing with these issues often becomes more complicated for us, too, because the issues we face have spent so long hidden in the shadows.

As a result, as a GBTQ guy, you have likely had a unique struggle that hasn't always been understood. But despite what society has undoubtedly told you, *there has never been anything wrong with you.*

You are fine, you are flawed, you are whole, and you are human.

That said, because of how the mind and brain work, there is a strong chance that a lot of the things you're struggling with today stem from your experiences of being different early on. Just about every mental health issue has "your environment" as a factor, and you're most vulnerable to that when you're young.

Environment affects your chances of having everything from depression and anxiety to PTSD and borderline personality disorder. (Not to mention a truly wide variety of physical health conditions.) When you are raised in an environment that isn't designed to appreciate, understand, or prioritize your whole self, that environment has set you up to fail. And your whole self is so complex. It's not just your sense of self, what you think of as "you," but also your identities, experiences, needs, stressors, fears, dreams, longings, desires, and so much more.

Furthermore, we live in a world that falsely blames us for all of our struggles with self-love and mental wellness, and refuses to acknowledge the complexity of our environments. We're taught that struggling with mental health is a moral and personal failure—that if we were just good enough, just "normal" enough, or just religious enough, we wouldn't be suffering.

Let me tell you unequivocally: This is not true. Society has taught us lies.

When society teaches us such incorrect and painful things, it becomes more and more difficult to get our needs met and heal ourselves—especially if our needs and wounds are less common, and therefore less frequently understood.

For example, when society teaches us that if we can't love ourselves, we can't truly love others, that turns a vital opportunity for healing into a source of chronic invalidation.

In truth, we can only learn to love ourselves when we receive love and affection in environments that don't try to force us to be people and things that we are not.

The basis of this book is the idea that gay, bi, trans, and queer guys have unique factors in our environments and our lives that affect our mental health and wellness. And in order to heal ourselves, we need to address the problems we actually have, by recognizing where the wounds began.

If you are a gay, bi, trans, or queer guy, this book is for you. Whether you've embraced these parts of who you are openly, are exploring what they mean to you, or are still in the closet, this guide is crafted with your experiences in mind.

THE DETERMINANTS FRAMEWORK

There are, unfortunately, many types of mental health problems out there, and no one is immune to getting them. Depression, anxiety, shame, low self-esteem, negative body image, and problem substance use—these are things that can affect anyone, regardless of their sexuality or gender identity. If you're reading this, you've probably struggled with some of them yourself.

However, just because everyone can experience these problems doesn't mean that we all experience them the same way. Each of these issues shows up differently for different people, depending on a lot of different factors, including a person's social and physical environment, as well as their experiences of privilege, power, and oppression.

These mental health issues also have different levels of intensity for different people. One major reason for this is that the stress of being marginalized—of social and familial rejection, of having to be so guarded, and of worse prospects in jobs, health, and most other areas—intensifies just about every mental health problem. That greater stress then mixes with the various norms, beliefs, values, and practices of all the communities that you belong to.

When stress shows up differently, it often needs to be dealt with differently—which is what this book aims to do.

In order to do that, this book draws on a framework—developed by the World Health Organization (WHO) and increasingly well-known among health policy experts and healthcare providers—called the "social determinants of health." As you might gather from the name, social determinants are the social factors that can lead to—or help determine—health inequalities. The WHO's framework looked specifically at physical health—but here, we're going to look at the determinants of our *mental* health outcomes.

So, what are the specific factors that determine GBTQ guys' mental well-being? This guidebook is divided into fifteen chapters, each one about a key driver in mental health—factors like social context, family and culture, our connections to others, and more—and the unique ways they show up in GBTQ communities. Meanwhile, we'll see how our mental health and well-being are very much shaped by the stress of living under dominant heterosexual, cisgender cultural norms—and by the possibilities and challenges that arise in the various queer subcultures we belong to.

Of course, each group and each individual within the GBTQ spectrum has a distinct story. We are not all alike—and that diversity makes us all the more beautiful. I would argue that difference is vital to what it means to be queer—certainly, it is vital to the fabric of humanity—and I would never want to erase those differences. When I address the gay, bisexual, trans, and queer men's communities together in this book, I do not mean to imply that we are all the same, nor that we *should* all be the same. Some of these topics may well not apply to you, or may feel less resonant for you, depending on your own identities, circumstances, and history. If so, you are more than welcome to skip ahead to what does feel relevant or call out to you.

Yet for all our differences, we share much in common as well. There are reasons our communities have banded together historically, as well as in the present. Those commonalities run throughout this book, as do our differences. We are united by many things, including the common threads of navigating life while feeling different and of living under a society that often assumes heterosexuality and cisgender identity are considered the norm—or worse, the only option. As GBTQ guys, we each have unique but often overlapping challenges, and this book intends to honor and address both our similarities and our differences. My hope is that this guidebook can facilitate our exploration of these shared narratives, fostering solidarity and support in our journeys toward mental well-being.

So, no matter how you identify, I truly hope this book can help you on your own journey. You deserve to feel happy and well and at peace with yourself and your communities. So, no matter whether you struggle with the burden of coming out or the fear of rejection, the pain of being different or the often-brutal judgments of hookup apps, I hope this book has something for you. Something that speaks to you and can help you heal.

WHAT TO EXPECT

In each chapter of this guidebook, we'll start by naming and talking about the specific issue—the determinant—that the chapter is going to explore. That's the start of the "educational" section of each chapter, because it's true what they say: knowledge *is* power. By understanding how each factor—such as shame, body image, masculinity, or sexual health—affects you, you'll learn how to take charge of your thoughts and emotions around that issue and help yourself feel better.

Each chapter uses a mix of structured and open-ended exercises that will give you the chance to dig into how you feel and why you feel that way—and how to get to the place you want to be. These exercises draw on a few different therapies:

1. Cognitive behavioral therapy (CBT) is based on the idea that our thoughts, feelings, and behaviors are always connected. Therefore, if we want to change how we feel, we can do that by changing our thoughts and actions. (And vice versa.)

2. Gestalt therapy is centered around the idea of "making successful contact." This means connecting with our embodied experience (which includes both our emotions and our physical sensations) while staying grounded in the present, so that we can live more authentically.

3. Psychodynamic therapy is about exploring connections between our past and present. It emphasizes the effect of things that happened during our early childhood and the ways we experienced the people, communities, and especially authority figures around us. It also speculates about the unconscious motivations behind our actions.

Let's try an exercise from one of these therapies, CBT, to give you a sense of what this book's exercises will be like.

THOUGHT ANALYSIS

Understanding your own thoughts and feelings isn't easy. Have you ever spent days feeling crappy for no reason—only to realize that you're upset about something your friend said or a rude comment from your boss? If you have, you know that what's happening inside you isn't always clear.

Luckily, figuring out your own thoughts and feelings is a skill—and that means that it's something you can *practice*. Here's a guide for how we're going to do that in this book, using a method called thought analysis:

1. **Situation:** Note the specific situation that is bringing up a difficult feeling for you.

2. **Feelings and behaviors:** List your feelings, rate their intensity from 1–10, and observe any behaviors you've carried out in response to the situation.

3. **Prominent unhelpful thought:** Identify your immediate automatic thoughts about the situation, particularly the "hot thought" that feels most prominent or powerful.

4. **Evaluate:** Focusing on that "hot thought," write down evidence that supports the thought, and then write down evidence that does *not* support the thought.

5. **Balanced alternative thought:** Come up a new thought that is more helpful while still being realistic (and not overly positive). Then, reassess the intensity of your feelings afterward to see if you feel better (even slightly).

Here's a brief thought analysis for Greg, a gay man who's contemplating going to a support group.

1. **Situation:** I'm contemplating finding a support group. I'm gay, forty-three, and experiencing anxiety about my sexuality at work.

2. **Feelings and behaviors:** Apprehension, uncertainty. I've researched groups and sought friends' advice, but for some reason I'm still reluctant to actually go.

3. **Prominent unhelpful thought:** Going to a support group means I can't take care of myself and I could lose my independence.

4. **Evaluate:** On the one hand, I've seen friends develop a dependency on groups, and media portrayals reaffirm this for me. On the other hand, I've heard positive stories from friends about the process, and I can stop going if I want.

5. **Balanced alternative thought:** A support group can be one of many ways I take care of myself. I can give it a try; it's not something I'm stuck with. And if something at work feels judgmental or homophobic, it would be nice to have group support in place.

As you can see, the goal of thought analysis is to help you slowly walk through your own thoughts and fears. Often, you have to start by figuring out what your thoughts even are, which thought analysis is designed to help with. We often feel things from deep in our subconscious, without knowing exactly what we're feeling or why. And we often act without recognizing what thoughts or feelings are driving us to behave the way we do.

Thoughts and feelings are intrinsically connected. Thus, one of the ways to change your thoughts is to try to change your feelings—and one of the most effective ways to change your feelings is to change your thoughts. This is yet another reason that knowing what your thoughts actually are is helpful.

Once you know what you're actually thinking, under it all, that's when the magic starts to happen. You can start to understand your thoughts and feelings about a given situation, what's influencing them, how they might be influencing each other, and whether or not they're accurate.

We stress out over misconceptions and misunderstandings all the time. For example, if you do something embarrassing—say, realizing halfway through your day that your shirt is inside out—it's so easy to think that everyone's been staring at you and judging you.

But actually, when you look at the evidence, human beings notice and remember way fewer things than we think. One of the best illustrations of this is an experiment shown in almost every Psychology 101 class: the invisible gorilla experiment (Chabris and Simons 2011).

This classic experiment starts with a video of players bouncing a basketball back and forth for a few minutes. During this experiment, the researchers ask participants to watch the basketball and count how many times it is passed back and forth. Then, in the middle of the video, a person in a full-body gorilla costume walks through the frame, right past the players, gorilla mask and all.

The vast majority of people watching the video never even see the gorilla, because they're so focused on the task they've been asked to complete.

So, if you're feeling embarrassed because you think everybody is staring at you, one way to calm yourself and lessen your feelings of embarrassment is to think about the gorilla experiment: most of the people around you probably haven't noticed a thing.

And that is exactly the type of thought we want here—a thought that contradicts or disproves the ones that your brain is freaking out about. "Everyone is judging me" is a thought that causes feelings of embarrassment. "I bet almost nobody noticed" is a much less stressful thought! That thought doesn't promote embarrassment—it *calms* embarrassment. It might even bring up feelings like amusement or satisfaction.

And just like that, your thoughts have changed the intensity of your emotions!

This works for just about any situation that brings up difficult feelings if you can get to the *hot thought*—the real, possibly secret thought or fear at the core of it all. Identifying the hot thought is itself a moment of recognition and relief because at that stage, you've decluttered your mind enough to get some clarity about what is driving your difficult feelings.

In the thought analysis we just looked at together, Greg's hot thought is "Going to a support group means I can't take care of myself and will lose my independence." Loss of independence is a very understandable fear! And for many people—especially GBTQ guys, with the rejection and lack of resources that we're more likely to face (Medina and Mahowald 2023)—it's a fear that can have horribly high stakes.

YOUR MENTAL HEALTH MATTERS

Whether you've been to a support group or not, you've picked up this guidebook to help you on your personal journey. Recognize that as a GBTQ individual, you've likely navigated unique challenges and societal misunderstandings. Despite any external messages, remember that nothing is inherently wrong with you. Your mental health struggles are valid and natural responses to unsupportive and uncertain environments. This book is tailored for you, embracing the diversity of your experiences and identities, and the nuances of our queer subcultures. It will serve as a supportive tool, guiding you through the journey toward mental wellness, grounded in the understanding that the issues faced by GBTQ individuals are complex and multifaceted, requiring a thoughtful approach to healing and self-acceptance.

DIGGING DEEPER

Greg might also benefit from psychodynamic inquiry. These are questions that explore the impact of earlier experiences, familial attachments, and other subconscious whispers. Here are some questions for Greg (that you might also find useful) to reflect on:

1. What would the people in your family of origin say about going to a support group if they were given the chance to go themselves?

2. Have you ever tried to talk about your mental health, only to be confronted with stigma or prejudice? What happened? What feelings did you walk away with?

3. Do you worry that using this book—or going to a group, or investing in your mental health in other ways—will be an admission that something is wrong with you? Or that the thing that's supposedly wrong in you is somehow connected to your queerness?

4. Many GBTQ guys have overdeveloped their self-reliance skills as a survival strategy. Might accessing a group or similar resources feel like you've failed at taking control of your life and its challenges?

Part 1

YOUR SOCIAL CONTEXT

Chapter 1

COMING OUT

In this chapter, we will consider multiple layers of the coming-out experience. It's a layered and complex process; it's also not something you'll do with everyone. Regardless of who you decide to share your sexual or gender identity with, the consideration, pressure, and lasting imprint around this experience is important to consider as a determinant of GBTQ mental health.

What's your relationship to the concept of coming out? Is it something you've already done, at least with some people in your life? Is it something you're still contemplating doing? Or perhaps you navigated the matter of coming out, in the way you saw fit, a long time ago. Whatever your situation, you can likely appreciate that there are implications for mental health and well-being. Let's examine the different kinds of choices a person might make—and the multiple coming-outs we might have during our lives—more closely. Some sections in this chapter might speak to you deeply, and others might not speak to you much at all. Either way, be open to what might emerge—or feel free to move to the next chapter, if you'd prefer.

Case Scenario: Rohan

Rohan *is bright, talented, seventeen years old, South Asian, and a guy from a conservative family of Pakistani descent, with strong traditional values. Throughout his life, Rohan has struggled with his sexual orientation, trying to come to terms with being gay. His friends are an integral part of his life, and he values their support and companionship immensely. However, he has never revealed his true identity to anyone before, and he is nervous about how they will react if he comes out.*

He's always monitoring his behavior, likes, dislikes, and all contributions to group conversations to avoid suspicion. He wants to be himself around his friends, but the idea scares him.

One evening, Rohan gathers the courage to talk to his closest friend, Aisha, who he feels would be the most understanding and accepting. Her response: "I'm glad you told me. You know, I kind of guessed it anyway. Your eyebrows are too fabulous for heterosexuality!"

As the days go by, Rohan starts opening up to a few more friends and acquaintances, and he receives support and love from a few. But mostly, the reception isn't so kind. For example, one person said, "I feel bad for your parents. I bet they wanted grandchildren." Another person said, "How do you know, dude? Have you hooked up with girls?" A third friend, one whom Rohan had felt kind of close to before, said, "The person you really need to talk to is God. You need to fix things—people like that go to hell." These comments were heartbreaking, and Rohan decided he wouldn't tell his parents until after he got into a university and could move away.

As you can see in Rohan's story, coming out isn't easy and comes with lots of uncertainties. It's also not a singular event, but rather a process, and one that moves in several stages.

COMING OUT TO YOURSELF

Despite cultural strides toward queer visibility, like Pride, there is a baseline presumption in much of society that people are heterosexual and cisgender until they say otherwise. And many of us grew up in family structures that are more or less nuclear and conventional. As a result, most GBTQ people endure at least some stress from isolated self-discovery—having to come to terms with their gender and sexual identity on their own—and struggle with the weight of "harboring a secret" about their identity. This usually begins with some tacit knowledge of being different and not fitting into rigidly gendered spaces.

The process of coming out to yourself, of understanding and accepting your own identity, is an important developmental stage that often gets overlooked. It can include any number of experiences, including exploring the language for GBTQ identities and confidently applying it to yourself, seeing representations of these identities in your environment, scrolling pornography to see what excites you, and working through the initial discomfort that can sometimes be present in being around other GBTQ people, especially if they challenge gender roles and boundaries more than you've been able to.

Coming out to yourself may also include periods of grieving. To be clear, cultural milestones like marriage and having children are ones queer and trans people have every right to pursue and absolutely do achieve. But there may be loss in acknowledging that the planning, experience, and celebration of these milestones may look or be different than if you were straight or cisgender.

DIGGING DEEPER

1. Did you once, or do you currently, pair your queerness with secrecy? If so, what parts of or people in your environment suggested this was necessary?

2. If you imagine the nuclear family to be a metaphorical closet, how would you describe the social and emotional conditions inside that closet (whether past or present)?

3. Reflect on the process of coming out to yourself. Where do you (or did you) seek information and resources? Were there other GBTQ people who initially made you uncomfortable, but whom you now appreciate as helpful role models?

4. How has (or might) being able to access sexual health information and services specific to GBTQ guys support your own sense of self?

COMING OUT TO OTHERS

When queer people consider coming out to others, their hesitation is often about the fear of rejection. Even if you feel that your family, circle of friends, or religious community is progressive and accepting, the possibility of rejection may loom, which can make the process of coming out an exercise in social risk-taking. Preparing for a loss of social and material support can be very scary. In fact, whether you've developed a personality that is fiercely self-reliant, one that longs for unconditional love, or you regularly fear a partner will leave you, any of these may be present-day responses that are connected to anticipating rejection early in life.

BEING OUTED WITHOUT CONSENT

Many GBTQ guys have had the awful experience of being outed without their consent. A friend of a friend may have shared the information you trusted them with; perhaps a parent or sibling found compromising pictures on your phone. You might have been outed by association after being tagged in a social media post. These breaches of privacy could easily have long-term emotional repercussions. For example, you might be cautious about sharing any information about yourself, you may regularly question whether people are trustworthy or not, or you may have also developed a core belief that "people will hurt me or leave me if they know the real me."

Some people will have experienced very real material and social losses as a result of their experience of coming out or being outed as GBTQ. Unfortunately, it's not uncommon for sexual and gender minorities to be silenced or disowned by their families, forced to endure conversion therapy or change efforts, or financially cut off from their guardians. These experiences are traumatic and can have a lasting impact on emotions, thinking styles, and coping strategies.

You might find your emotions moving from curious, vulnerable, hopeful, or shy to angry, on edge, disappointed, depressed, or hypervigilant against threat. You might find your thoughts of your own self-worth and the worth of building relationships with others are impacted, with thoughts like *I'm unlovable* or *People will let me down*. You might find your ideas of your future altered, with new pressure to think small, think "survival," or avoid big risks. And finally, your behavior might be affected: you might find yourself anxious, isolated, losing interest in things that once felt vital to you, or using substances to escape or as your sole way to connect to others.

DIGGING DEEPER

1. If you anticipated rejection from others, what did you mentally prepare to lose? How did that preparatory headspace leave a lasting imprint on your personality and connection to others?

2. If your family structure was less nuclear normative (through extended/blended family, adoption, foster home, stepparents, step/half siblings), how did that structure influence your thoughts about what coming out might look like?

COMING OUT AS TRAUMATIC

Coming out can be a profound and sometimes traumatic event in the life of GBTQ guys. While some may navigate this experience without lasting negative effects, for others, the repercussions can resonate deeply, altering their perception of self, others, and the future. Cognitive behavioral theories suggest that traumatic events like a difficult coming out can lead to fundamental changes in core beliefs, emotions, and behaviors. These shifts can profoundly impact well-being and the ability to cope.

To illustrate this transformation, let's use the Affect-Behavior-Cognition (ABC) Analysis to delve into the shifts that occurred for Rohan after his coming-out experience, particularly the negative reactions.

BEFORE COMING OUT

Affect and emotions: Rohan was curious, vulnerable, hopeful, and social.

Behavior and coping: Rohan engaged in art, cycling, reading, rested well, and enjoyed socializing with others. He used substances occasionally for fun and as a means to connect with people.

Cognition and core beliefs:

Self: Rohan believed he was worthy.

Others/world: He felt that people were worth building friendships with.

Future: Rohan was optimistic about the future, believing he could dream and try again even if he fell.

AFTER COMING OUT

Affect and emotions: Rohan was sad, on edge, and hypervigilant.

Behavior and coping: He became a bit more isolated and anxious, lost interest in some activities. His ambition and dreaming were reduced, and substance use became a means of escape and his main way to connect with others.

Cognition and core beliefs:

>Self: He saw himself as unlovable and a source of pain.

>Others/world: He felt that people would ultimately let him down.

>Future: His outlook became constrained to thinking small and focusing on survival, avoiding any significant risks.

These changes underscore the potential impact of coming out as a traumatic event, highlighting the importance of understanding and support during and after this critical life experience. Consider doing an ABC analysis for yourself to reflect on the ways coming-out experiences may have shifted your affect, behaviors, and cognitions. You can find a blank copy of the ABC analysis here: http://www.newharbinger.com/55039.

DIGGING DEEPER

1. If coming out was a traumatic event or experience for you, how did it shift your emotions, thoughts, and behaviors?

2. What personal level of control and choice did you have through the process of coming out? (If applicable.) How did that influence your personality and connection to others?

FROM COMING OUT TO INVITING IN

It's clear that coming out puts a lot of pressure on queer people. And the stakes are often quite high. More recently, advocates have been suggesting a shift from *coming out* to *inviting in* (Johns 2020). This shift recognizes that the pressure to come out can put people in situations that are physically or psychologically unsafe. Conversely, inviting people to know particular parts of your identity gives you, the GBTQ person, much more control over who knows what. Inviting in can be seen as much more empowering than coming out. Further, coming out has been critiqued as a concept steeped in dominant Western culture, one that requires family acceptance to be explicit and paired with outward declarations of pride, which doesn't fit the cultural scripts of many non-white communities (Sanchez 2017). Some religious communities also associate the language of pride with sinfulness because it negates the role of a higher being in human achievements, emphasizing the individual person.

GBTQ guys who have endured significant psychological pain during their coming-out process, followed by liberation and reduced shame, may hesitate to welcome those who haven't had similar experiences into their circles. This perspective, both judgmental and self-protective, can stem from only seeing a single path forward for queer identity in a predominantly straight world, as well as a desire to distance themselves from "closet life."

As a GBTQ person, you'll have to decide what model of sharing personal information works best for you.

Digging Deeper

1. What path do you want to choose, or have you already chosen? What led you to that decision?

2. If you are selectively out, and have perhaps embraced the concept of *inviting in*, have you experienced judgment or exclusion from other queer people? If yes, how have you made sense of it?

AWARENESS EXERCISE: VISUALIZATION

Reflecting on our thoughts and feelings can be really tiring work! Healing can certainly take other forms as well. The next exercise is designed to let you use less thinking power and more imagination and self-observation. The goal is simply to notice how you feel in your body throughout the exercise.

Read through the following guided imagery script and visualize each step.

Close your eyes, take a deep breath, and let yourself relax.

Imagine you are a twelve-year-old boy hidden in the dark, cramped space of your bedroom closet. You can hear the muffled sounds of your parents arguing outside, their voices rising and falling. The worry gnaws at you—what if someone gets hurt? What if someone leaves?

The door creaks open and light spills in. You see the shadows of your older brother and his friends. They're laughing, unaware of you. You shrink back, not wanting to be seen or judged.

Focus on your breathing. It's shallow, quick. Now, slowly, start taking deeper breaths. Feel your chest rise and fall. With each breath, you feel a bit more in control, a bit more at peace.

Why are you hiding? What are you afraid of? You ponder these questions, feeling the weight of your secret. What would happen if your family knew?

Your breathing deepens. You feel your chest expand, gently touching the closet door. Your hands press against the wood, ready to push it open.

Pause. Shift your thoughts. You're not just hiding a secret—you're preparing for a surprise party. Your secret, your queerness, is not something to be ashamed of. It's a part of the beautiful surprise that is you.

Imagine yourself throwing open the closet door. Confetti bursts into the air, showering you in a rainbow of colors. You step out, a wide smile on your face.

Continue to breathe deeply, savoring the feeling of liberation. You walk through your house, each step more confident than the last. The confetti follows you, a colorful trail marking your path.

Step outside. Your neighborhood is alive with clapping and cheering. People are celebrating you, just as you are. The confetti swirls around you, a symbol of joy and acceptance.

Finally, you pause. You turn back to the closet, your former hiding place. Thank it for its shelter, for giving you the time and space you needed. You realize how much you've grown, how ready you are now for this celebration of your true self.

Take a final deep breath. Feel the pride and joy swell in your heart. When you're ready, slowly open your eyes, bringing a piece of this confidence and self-acceptance back into your world.

As you open your eyes, take a moment to ground yourself back in the present, carrying the strength and courage from your imagery with you.

REFLECTIONS

1. As you visualized stepping out of the closet into a celebration, what emotions surfaced for you? Did you experience resistance, joy, or disbelief? How did these feelings compare to the emotions you felt while imagining hiding in the closet?

2. This exercise shifts from a place of fear to one of celebration. How does that change in narrative affect your perception of your own coming-out experience? The idea of coming out in general?

3. As you reflect on thanking the closet for its shelter, what insights do you gain about the role of protective mechanisms in your life?

DECISIONAL BALANCE

Welcome to another key step in your self-help journey: the decisional balance. Here, we shift from reflecting on the process of coming out to learning tools you can use to help you make intentional choices.

Decisional balance is a tool that comes from a type of therapy called motivational interviewing. It's designed to support behavior change, and can also assist you in evaluating the pros and cons of a decision, helping you gain a clearer, more balanced perspective on how to move forward. You can also use it to determine how to proceed when it comes to inviting more people into your inner world.

Below, you will find a sample of a decisional balance activity, for a hypothetical queer guy reflecting on the prospect of "inviting more people in." The exercise begins with listing the benefits and costs of not changing (not letting people in), followed by the costs and benefits of making a change (letting people in).

1. Benefits of not changing:
   - I can avoid other people's judgments.
   - I won't need to answer people's questions.
   - All of my current friendships will remain intact.
   - Harmony in my family.

2. Costs of not changing:

    - It's harder to meet other GBTQ people; I'm apprehensive about going to events.

    - I'll continue to worry about being outed by association.

    - If I pursue a relationship, it will have to be hidden.

3. Cost of making a change:

    - I'll have to face some uncertainty in all relationships, including family.

    - Anxiety, emotional exhaustion.

    - Possible rejection.

    - Might be faced with uncomfortable questions.

4. Benefits of making a change:

    - I might feel lighter.

    - I could experience deeper acceptance.

    - Meeting other GBTQ people might get easier.

    - I'll be less anxious about managing information and social media.

You'll notice that there is a close link between the benefits of not changing and the costs of making a change (numbers one and three) on one hand, and the costs of not changing and the benefits of making a change (numbers two and four). In a sense, the linked elements in this process speak directly to one another. (This might be more apparent in the visual chart, which you can access at the website for this book, http://www.newharbinger.com/55039.)

You might be wondering why anyone would ask about the benefits of not making a change. We have to appreciate that not changing likely represents the most immediate psychological safety for a lot of people. Likewise, the benefits of making a change are usually longer-term outcomes that can feel hard to appreciate in the moment, but are useful to imagine. That's why we get to them last—it takes time to get there!

Would it be useful to you to complete your own decisional balance chart to evaluate the change of inviting more people in—or any other change you're contemplating? If yes, visit http://www.newharbinger.com/55039 for a decisional balance worksheet you can complete, now or any time you might need to.

THE EMPTY CHAIR EXPERIENCE

The Empty Chair exercise is one of the most distinctive and powerful tools in Gestalt therapy. It is designed to create a dialogue between different parts of the self, or between the self and an imagined other. In this exercise, one chair represents you, and the empty chair represents another person, an aspect of yourself, or a symbolic figure. The objective is to either speak directly to the empty chair for a one-sided conversation, or alternate between the chairs, engaging in a two-sided conversation. This method is particularly effective for addressing deep-seated emotions, conflicts, and unresolved issues.

In this section, you are invited to engage in a unique adaptation of the Empty Chair exercise, specifically designed to navigate the sensitive and significant topic of coming out as GBTQ. Identify someone in your life whom you didn't have the opportunity to come out to or whom you don't think you'd want to invite in to your queerness. The person could be alive, or perhaps they've passed and you have some unfinished business, or perhaps they're alive but no longer in your life, for whatever reason. For example, you may identify a grade school teacher who had a significant impact on you or a family member that you're estranged from.

This conversation, while it may never occur in real life, holds substantial internal importance. Engaging in this dialogue aloud, even in an imagined context, serves several therapeutic purposes. First, it allows you to give voice to unexpressed emotions and thoughts, facilitating a deeper understanding of your inner landscape. Second, it provides an opportunity to empathize with the perspective of the other, even if that other is a part of yourself. Last, this exercise can offer a sense of resolution or closure, helping you reconcile internal conflicts and move forward with greater clarity and self-acceptance.

Whether you choose to do this alone, with a friend, or in the presence of a therapist, the Empty Chair exercise offers a safe and structured environment to express, explore, and understand your feelings and thoughts about this deeply personal subject. I encourage you to approach this with an open heart and mind, embracing the opportunity to articulate and explore feelings and thoughts that might have remained unexpressed. By participating in this exercise, you aim to achieve a deeper understanding of yourself, a sense of peace with unexpressed realities, and a step forward in your journey of self-exploration and acceptance.

To set up an Empty Chair exercise, follow these basic steps:

STEP 1: CREATE THE SPACE

- Choose a space where you feel safe and will not be interrupted. This environment should feel comfortable and allow you to express yourself freely.

- Place two chairs opposite each other, a few feet apart. One chair represents you, and the other represents the person you are talking to.

- Take a few moments to center yourself. Breathe deeply and think about the topic you want to address. In this case, it's a conversation about your sexual/gender identity, with someone with whom such a conversation cannot realistically take place.

STEP 2: SPEAK TO THE EMPTY CHAIR

- Sit in one chair to start the dialogue. Speak as if you are talking directly to the person represented by the empty chair. Express your feelings, thoughts, and questions openly and honestly.

- Take a moment to think about if there's anything left to say. Be okay with moving slowly, and when you're sure you're done, then switch. It's also okay if everything doesn't get said. Once you feel like you've gotten a lot off your chest, pause for a moment, and decide whether you want to stay in that chair or want to switch.

STEP 3: SWITCH CHAIRS AND EMBODY THE OTHER ENTITY

- When ready, switch to the empty chair, taking the perspective of the other person. Respond to what you just said, imagining what their reactions, feelings, and words might be.

- Alternate between the chairs, continuing the dialogue, and exploring different aspects of the conversation. Go slow. Feel every part of the experience.

STEP 4: CONCLUSION

- When you feel the conversation has reached a natural end, or you've expressed all you need to, conclude the exercise and allow yourself to continue reflecting on how this experience felt in your body.

Once you've finished the exercise, take a moment to reflect on the experience by answering the following questions.

1. What insights did you gain from imagining the other person's responses?

2. Think about how you perceived the other person's reactions and responses during the role-play. What does this tell you about your fears, hopes, or expectations regarding their acceptance and understanding of your identity?

3. How did embodying their perspective change your view of the situation?

4. How did embodying your own perspective bring you closer to understanding your unmet needs?

CONCLUSION

As you reach the end of this chapter, reflect on the journey that you have had to navigate. This chapter has taken us through various terrains—the introspective path of self-recognition, the external challenges of societal norms, and the intimate disclosures to loved ones.

The process of grappling with coming out touches every facet of your life, influencing your mental health and overall well-being. Hopefully, the exercises you've engaged with have prompted you to examine your unhelpful thinking patterns, explore decision-making, and reflect on the potential trauma of coming out. The experiential exercises will have encouraged you to sit with the embodied emotion that comes with visualizations and role-play.

As you prepare to step into the next chapter, carry forward the awareness that coming out happens within a societal context that can sometimes be hostile. Homophobia, biphobia, and transphobia are realities that you may have experienced. The next chapter will confront these harsh realities, digging into their roots, how they present themselves in your life, and their impact on the mental health of GBTQ individuals like you.

Chapter 2

HOMOPHOBIA, BIPHOBIA, TRANSPHOBIA

Welcome to an essential chapter in this book, dedicated to exploring the complex and multifaceted issues of homophobia, biphobia, and transphobia, and their impacts on the mental health of gay, bisexual, trans, and queer guys.

Let's start with some definitions. Homophobia refers to the fear, hatred, discomfort with, or mistrust of people who are gay. Biphobia is a similar aversion toward bisexuality and bisexual people, often based on stereotypes, misconceptions, and misunderstandings about bisexuality. Transphobia encompasses a range of negative attitudes, feelings, and actions toward transgender people and toward anything that generally challenges the gender binary. Each of these phobias can manifest in various forms, from explicit violence and discrimination to subtler forms of prejudice and microaggressions.

It's also useful to know about and recognize heteronormativity and cisnormativity—words for the assumption that everyone is heterosexual and cisgender unless they state otherwise. This worldview, built into every facet of society, treats heterosexual and cisgender identities as the default (i.e., normal, natural, and neutral), marginalizing and othering GBTQ individuals. Simply navigating the everyday world can come with environmental and interpersonal microaggressions.

When cisgender and heterosexual identities are considered the default, other expressions of gender and sexual or romantic attraction are met with questions about causes ("How did you become this way?"), stereotypes ("Aren't all gay men feminine?"), failure narratives ("You're so attractive; your babies would be beautiful—what a waste!"), and morality ("Do you think God will accept you the way you are?"). Each of these questions comes with psychological consequences for those of us subjected to them.

While the legalization of same-sex marriage and the increased representation of GBTQ individuals in media have marked significant strides in social acceptance and visibility, it's crucial to acknowledge that negative attitudes and prejudices toward our communities remain deeply ingrained in many parts of the world, including "progressive" countries. The enduring presence of these phobias can have a profound impact on our mental health. It can contribute to feelings of isolation, anxiety, depression, and a decreased sense of self-worth.

In this chapter, we'll explore how these phobias may have affected your life—from queerphobic microaggressions to emotionally and physically violent attacks. And we'll aim to foster a sense of empowerment and resilience, helping you use therapeutic skills to navigate a world that is still learning to embrace the full spectrum of human diversity. Let's begin this journey by understanding these phobias and the ways in which they can generate lasting fears and disrupt opportunities for belonging. Our therapeutic tools in this chapter will include CBT problem solving, a Gestalt experiment with speaking to your inner child, and psychodynamic inquiry to help you dig deeper on the impact of what you may have already had to endure.

MICROAGGRESSIONS

Harvard psychiatrist Chester Pierce first described microaggressions as offensive behaviors that were experienced as "subtle and stunning" (1970). Take a moment to think about the word "offensive." A defense mechanism—whether avoidance, denial, or increased motivation—is a subconscious strategy intended to protect us from difficult or upsetting feelings. It then follows that an offense mechanism would operate by attacking another person (the opposite of protecting) in a subconscious way to create difficult feelings in others.

Homophobia, biphobia, and transphobia are commonly expressed as microaggressions. In this section, we will explore microaggressions against GBTQ people, and at times we will use the term queerphobia to refer to collective experiences.

Can you recall specific experiences of microaggressions—small or casual statements or actions that reveal discrimination toward you and dismissal of or hostility toward your identity—based on your gender or sexual identity? Perhaps you have multiple minority identities, which interact, compound, and fold into one another in everyday life. Are you ever given time and space to exist with your gender identity or sexual orientation treated as a neutral fact, or is it something you're continually compelled to be aware of?

See if any of the following case scenarios resonate with your experience.

Michael is a thirty-two-year-old, Black, Caribbean, Canadian man who works as a marketing manager at an advertising agency. He was excited to represent bisexuality on his company's Pride panel, an opportunity to share his unique perspectives. However, his excitement dimmed when his sister said she was surprised he would focus on bisexuality, given his recent relationships with men. This is a common biphobic microaggression: the invalidation of bisexuality based on the gender of one's current partner, which suggests a binary view of sexuality that erases the fluidity and legitimacy of bisexual identity (Fredrick 2017).

Another time, Michael and his friend Jordan went to a queer dance party. Both Black and bisexual, they were questioned by the bouncer: "You guys are aware that this is an LGBT event?" It was a clear instance of intersectional bias and microaggressions. This questioning assumed they were outsiders to the queer space and highlighted racial stereotypes—that Black people and people of color are often assumed to be straight, amplifying feelings of erasure.

Kaiden, a white transgender man in his early twenties, was at the campus pub, splitting a plate of nachos and a pint with a pal after a game of squash. One of Kaiden's classmates spotted them and came to say hello. The classmate had learned that Kaiden was trans after he shared something personal during a class discussion. At the pub, the classmate suddenly began probing Kaiden with personal questions about his body and transition process. Kaiden was able to deflect some of this but felt uncomfortable. Unfortunately, Kaiden is used to this. Denial of bodily privacy is a common microaggression against trans people (Nadal et al. 2012).

Fanuel, a gay man in his forties living with HIV, was shaken after reading a recent news article. It talked about someone who was incarcerated for not disclosing their HIV status before a sexual encounter. This news hit close to home for Fanuel, who had spent years combating stigma and advocating for accessible treatment within his community. The law, he realized, perpetuated the harmful stereotype that gay men's sexuality is inherently dangerous, undermining progress toward equality and understanding. Gay men living with HIV often experience compounding microaggressions around sexuality (Eaton et al. 2020).

Take a moment to consider Michael, Kaiden, and Fanuel's experiences, and how they might connect with your own. And consider: If you were in a similar position, how might you advocate for yourself? How might you find ways to get your needs met or heal from the injury that others' mistreatment of you might cause?

Finally, how might you like to see society at large, or the spaces you're most frequently in, change, so that you don't have to experience this injury anymore?

CBT PROBLEM SOLVING

There's a common misperception that therapy, and CBT in particular, requires that people change their thinking styles, and that it's all about changing the way you think about situations rather than the situations themselves. Actually, you only need to identify and alter your automatic thoughts when you suspect they are unhelpful and holding you back. In cases where you face a difficult experience and your reading is factual—i.e., that was indeed a homophobic microaggression—you are then in a position to explore what you want to do and what will lead to the best outcomes for you. That means considering and evaluating all of your options before responding. Here's a problem-solving map for Michael.

- **Situation:** Michael says, "My sister questioned the legitimacy of my bisexuality because I've dated men."

- **Feelings:** Angry, frustrated, sad, and dismissed.

- **Thoughts:** I'll never be understood; I wish life didn't feel like a constant fight.

- **Problem:** People who are close to me should know better.

- **Goal:** I want people who are close to me to interact with me in a way that feels affirming.

- **Possible solutions:** I could get angry in the moment; I could write a letter to my sister; I could return to the conversation later and explain why her words were hurtful.

- **Evaluate solutions:** Getting angry won't communicate how she can be more affirming; writing a letter could work but feels like a lot of work; a conversation would be best for my communication style, but I worry she'll say she doesn't remember the details of our exchange.

- **Plan of action:** (a) Write down a few points I want to convey; (b) In particular, I want to make this point: "It feels like you (and others) are uncomfortable if I'm not in a neat box, and I want you to try and challenge this," and (c) find a time to have this conversation, because waiting too long will make things harder.

Is there a recent experience for which you might wish to use this process? When you complete this process of evaluation on your own, keep in mind that the distinction between situation, problem, and goal is crucial. The *situation* is about identifying the external context or event. The *problem* focuses on the specific challenge within the situation that you can influence or change. The *goal* is about envisioning the desired outcome or resolution to the problem identified.

When you evaluate all of your possible solutions to a given problem, you'll want to consider how each solution meets or doesn't meet your goal. You might find that your initial solution is being guided by your feelings and initial thoughts, rather than a clear goal, so it will likely leave you feeling unsatisfied.

You can try using this tool right away! A template can be found here: http://www.newharbinger.com/55039.

VIOLENT PHOBIAS

Microaggressions are often unpleasant and hurtful, but they often occur in relatively low-intensity situations. And typically, if you're on the receiving end, you can take a step back and reflect on how you want to approach them. The opportunity to take a step back is somewhat of a luxury next to the more violent expressions of homophobia, biphobia, and transphobia. As described in the previous chapter, experiences of trauma can change the way we perceive ourselves, others, the world, and our future.

If you've experienced violence resulting from your sexual or gender identity, you may find this next scenario triggering. That means you'll likely feel anxiety and tension in your body, as your own memories and experiences come back to visit you in the present moment. Take care of yourself as you read. Remind yourself that you are currently not in danger. In addition, remind yourself that reflecting on difficult experiences and engaging with them can reduce the intensity of your visceral responses over time (Julian et al. 2023). This is called narrative exposure therapy, which is rooted in the principles of trauma-focused CBT. You can also take a break now or anytime you might need to.

Case Scenario

Jae-Won, *a nineteen-year-old Korean American gay man, was visiting family in the city of Seoul, South Korea, for the summer. Raised in the United States, Jae-Won embraced his Korean heritage while living an openly gay life. It was his first time in Seoul since coming out, and he was eager to explore the city's LGBTQ+ scene.*

One evening, filled with excitement and curiosity, Jae-Won decided to visit a popular local gay bar. He dressed boldly: short shorts and a leather harness, celebrating his physique with confidence. The bar was perfect: queer and Korean. Jae-Won felt a sense of belonging like never before.

As the night progressed, Jae-Won danced and laughed with newfound friends, embracing the freedom of self-expression. But outside the safe confines of the bar, a storm was brewing.

As he made his way home after the bar closed, Jae-Won encountered a group of aggressive individuals. The moment they spotted Jae-Won, they hurled slurs and insults at him. The situation quickly escalated. Jae-Won was beaten that night before the assailants dispersed, leaving him to be found by strangers who helped him get to his hotel.

Word of the violent incident spread through the LGBTQ+ community in Seoul, sparking a surge of outrage and solidarity. The local LGBTQ+ organizations, bar owners, and allies united, holding a peaceful protest to condemn the act of violence. Social media platforms buzzed with supportive hashtags for Jae-Won, raising awareness of the harsh realities LGBTQ+ individuals face, even in progressive cities like Seoul.

Jae-Won felt supported, but this experience of homophobia kept replaying in his mind over and over. He feared that he might never be quite the same.

REFLECTIONS

Jae-Won's story represents the movement from microaggressions to homophobic violence. This is an intense experience. It's worth taking some time to process, perhaps in your journal.

- Can you recall experiences of explicit and outward queer/transphobia in your own life? How did you feel at the time? How do you feel in your body in this moment, as you recall those experiences?

- The cognitive behavioral therapy model posits that people who experience trauma also experience a shift in their beliefs about themselves, the world, and the future. Based on the scenario above, how might Jae-Won's views and perspectives shift after the violent experience (e.g., assumptions of safety, acceptance, visibility, etc.)?

- Have your experiences of queer/transphobia affected your sense of self and your core beliefs about yourself?

- When people are outwardly queer/transphobic, how do you make sense of their hate and disdain?

FEAR AND WELLNESS

As you've likely discovered over the previous sections, homophobia, biphobia, and transphobia can have a significant effect on your mental health. If you are regularly in proximity to possible violence, you'll notice that your mind and body are frequently in a vigilant state. Vigilance is a strong nervous system reaction to threats—and possible threats—in your environment.

While vigilance is a physiological response designed to keep you safe, it can be exhausting. It means you will have less energy to focus on school, work, friendships, hobbies, and other obligations. It could even mean that you don't experience restful sleep because you are anxious about the possible threats the following day.

Even if you've been able to find physical and psychological safety in your life, away from outward and violent queerphobia, your body will likely still carry memories of what it was like when you felt unsafe. It's important to have compassion for the part of you that still carries these fears of violence, particularly if it gets activated from time to time in everyday situations.

Beyond physical safety and the circumstances of day-to-day life, GBTQ people also have to be aware of many other experiences of discrimination and exclusion that are rooted in homophobia, biphobia, and transphobia. These can include, but are not limited to:

- Anti-LGBTQ+ propaganda by politicians and threats to rescind essential health services
- Assumptions of being heterosexual or cisgender
- Bi erasure—the experience of being made invisible in both straight and queer spaces as a bisexual person
- Denial of access to public facilities
- Discomfort in public spaces that are rigidly gendered
- Enduring someone else's process of grief after you've come out to them
- Others equating queerness with promiscuity and recklessness
- Hateful speech in the media and online
- Healthcare discrimination
- Gendered expectations in a family or culture
- Inadequate or insensitive healthcare services
- Inappropriate or invasive questions about sex, sexuality, relationships, and transition-related surgeries
- Misgendering and deadnaming
- Nonaffirming interpretations of religious theology
- Rejection or criticism from family and friends
- Stereotypes about being queer or trans
- Stigma and ostracization in religious communities
- Suggestions to change one's sexual or gender identity

Think about which of these applies to you, and feel free to write down your own. You might also take some time to journal about the experience—how it feels, the thoughts it inspires in you, and how you might be able to evaluate and challenge those thoughts to begin repairing any harm from these experiences.

Ultimately, there are two key things you should take away from this section. The first is that fear is a normal and appropriate response to all forms of queerphobia and transphobia. The second is that both past and ongoing experiences of fear will affect our mental health and well-being. For example, someone who experiences fear and exclusion regularly might isolate themselves, be more reserved, have difficulty sharing feelings, and might use drugs and alcohol to self-medicate for underlying anxiety.

DIGGING DEEPER

Consider the questions below. These can be useful to journal about, talk through with a trusted person, or simply reflect on. They are designed to help you think about your unconscious reactions.

1. Do you sometimes hold back to avoid possible rejection or discrimination? While this is sometimes necessary for safety, self-censorship (e.g., remaining silent, toning down your wardrobe) can create a gap between the person you want to be and the person you feel you have to be. How might this impact your self-esteem?

2. Have you found yourself getting angry with people who actually support you? For example, you might yell at a sibling or close friend, saying they don't know what you're going through, even though they've been with you every step of the way and didn't actually suggest they know exactly what your experience was. If so, this might be because a defense mechanism—specifically displacement—is trying to protect you after negative experiences. It would not have been safe to respond to your aggressor with this tone, so your anger finds a safer target.

BELONGING AND WELLNESS

In a 1943 paper titled "A Theory of Human Motivation," Abraham Maslow, an American psychologist, proposed a hierarchy of needs. The hierarchy forms a pyramid, with basic survival needs of food and shelter at the base, followed by safety, and then belonging. That's right, a sense of belonging is not a mere interest or luxury, but an actual human need. But what does belonging look like for GBTQ people—and more specifically, for you?

The exact answer is different for everyone. But generally, we tend to feel a sense of belonging when we have:

- Family acceptance
- Friendships
- Proximity to people with shared experiences
- Community and support networks
- Safe spaces to share our ideas and identities
- Freedom for authenticity and self-expression
- Accurate representations in media
- Supportive laws and policies in place around us
- Equitable access to opportunities for personal and professional growth

Which of these factors are present in your life? Perhaps you've met other GBTQ people who offer you a sense of belonging. Or perhaps your relationships with other friends or family members uplift you in your identity. Perhaps you have a creative practice or some other venue for self-expression that gives you a sense that you belong and are safe just as you are.

For GBTQ people, belonging can also come from having opportunities to heal from difficult experiences of homophobia, biphobia, and transphobia.

Ultimately, the current science is clear: a lack of belonging is connected to depression (Dutcher et al. 2022), anxiety (Moeller et al. 2020), and negative physical health outcomes (Hale et al. 2005).

Knowing all of this, we can start to map out a plan for optimizing our mental health as GBTQ guys. First, we can try to find safety to facilitate healing from queerphobia. Second, we can continually work toward cultivating a sense of belonging through groups, events, friendships, relationships, activism, and more. Finally, we can also use the skills we've learned to process experiences of queerphobia and trauma when they happen, so they don't impact our sense of belonging as intensely.

DIGGING DEEPER

Consider the questions below. These can be useful to journal about, talk through with a trusted person, or simply reflect on. They are designed to help you think about your unconscious process.

1. How has your family's acceptance or lack thereof shaped your sense of belonging and self-esteem?

2. Can you identify any conflicts between your desire for authenticity and self-expression, and your need for safety and belonging? How do you navigate these conflicts, and what does that process say about your way of being in the world?

3. Have you found yourself to be "over-attuned" to queerphobia at times? For example, you might mistake a neutral comment for a negative one. Or, you think everyone is looking at you, but after checking with a friend, you realize that's not the case. If so, this might be because a defense mechanism called projection is trying to protect you following negative experiences. Essentially, a past experience likely planted the seeds of insecurity in you, and now you look for echoes of that experience in other people. This can get in the way of belonging.

THE EMPTY CHAIR: YOUR INNER CHILD

Experiences of queerphobia can feel too big to tackle with a CBT tool. Instead, we can turn to ourselves and reconnect with parts of ourselves that are still afraid. Those parts of you need attention, reassurance, and compassion. I encourage you to approach this exercise with an open heart and mind, embracing the opportunity to articulate and explore feelings and thoughts that might have remained unspoken.

To set up this Empty Chair exercise, follow these basic steps:

Step 1: Create the Space

- Choose a space where you feel safe and will not be interrupted. This environment should feel comfortable and allow you to express yourself freely.

- Place two chairs opposite each other, a few feet apart. One chair represents you, and the other represents your inner child, with whom you are having the conversation.

- Take a few moments to center yourself. Breathe deeply and think about the topic you want to address. In this case, it's a conversation about your younger self (inner child) having to endure homophobia.

Step 2: Speak to Your Inner Child

- Sit in one chair to start the dialogue. Speak as if you are talking directly to the inner child represented by the empty chair. Express your feelings, thoughts, and questions openly and honestly.

Step 3: Switch Chairs and Embody your Inner Child

- When you feel ready, switch to the empty chair, taking the perspective of the other person—your inner child. Respond to what you just said, imagining what their reactions, feelings, and words might be.

- Alternate between the chairs, continuing the dialogue and exploring different aspects of the conversation. Go slow. Feel every part of the experience.

Step 4: Conclusion

- When you feel the conversation has reached a natural end, or you've expressed all you need to, conclude the exercise and allow yourself to continue reflecting on how it felt in your body.

REFLECTIONS

Once you've completed the activity, reflect on the experience in a journal.

- How was it helpful to have that conversation with your inner child? What part of your history did it remind you of?

- In what ways did this exercise bridge a connection between your experiences of pain and joy?

- What would it look like for you to continue with the journey of integrating your past and present selves?

CONCLUSION

In this chapter, we have delved into the pervasive and damaging effects of homophobia, biphobia, and transphobia. These forms of discrimination can be experienced as biases, subtle microaggressions, and overt acts of aggression. This incessant stream of negativity can erode one's sense of self, leading to a vigilant state that saps energy, diminishes self-worth, and leads to isolation. However, recognizing these patterns is the first step toward reclaiming your power.

As we transition to the next chapter, we will navigate the intricacies of shame—a profound and often petrifying experience that arises from internalizing these phobias. Shame is not merely a surface wound but rather a deep-seated scar affecting our consciousness, influencing how we see ourselves and interact with the world. By confronting shame head-on, we can begin to understand its roots in queerphobia and unravel its hold on our psyches.

Chapter 3

INTERNALIZED SHAME

Shame is a complex, socially mediated emotion that involves an internalized sense of personal deficiency—a feeling that you're "less than" or inferior. Unlike guilt, which comes from specific actions, shame suggests that one's entire self is fundamentally flawed or less than. This intense feeling of inadequacy can range from mild embarrassment to a pervasive sense of inferiority, where individuals believe they are inherently unworthy of acceptance or love (Thawer 2022).

INFERIORITY AND WELLNESS

In GBTQ communities, shame often relates to societal and familial expectations that do not affirm queer identities. Many GBTQ men encounter shame from an early age thanks to societal norms that punish or invalidate nonheteronormative expressions of identity. This shame can manifest in various ways, such as internalized negative perceptions of your sexuality, struggles with body image, or discomfort with self-advocacy. Ultimately, these experiences lead to a broader belief in your own inferiority, where your identity feels like a deficit rather than something to be celebrated (Thawer 2022).

Case Scenario

Jaime *is a Latinx gay guy in his late twenties, and in general, his life is going really well. He has a great, well-paying job as a software engineer. He's got a nice apartment right over a cute coffee shop, which he works from two days a week. He lives in a major city that thousands of people dream of moving to. He's even got a good social life—he gets along great with his roommate, plays pickup soccer with a group of guys he's gotten close with, and goes out for drinks with friends most weekends.*

Despite all that, Jaime still feels like there's something wrong with him. Something that he goes to a lot of pains to hide and that has stopped all his efforts to get out there and find a relationship.

Jaime is walking around with a heavy helping of secret shame over this: he hasn't been in a relationship in over ten years.

He hasn't hooked up with anyone since college, either, something that makes him feel like an outsider in the very hookup-heavy gay culture of the major city where he lives. He avoids a lot of clubs and parties too, even when he'd like to go—even though he knows it's probably not true, he feels like his years of accidental celibacy are hanging over him like a neon sign.

Jaime's feelings of shame are all too natural, given the different cultures and subcultures he lives in. From the dominant, straight culture, he's bombarded with messages saying that he needs a relationship to be whole, from bloggers to romcoms to some very stressful conversations with his aunts and uncles. And while the gay community he's found is a huge breath of fresh air when it comes to homophobia, he also witnesses their group's casual confession circles about their sexcapades, which makes him feel left out.

You might well be familiar with some of these feelings. Heteronormativity is so hard to escape, after all, and gay hookup apps are often a hotbed of judgment—especially if you're like Jaime, and are rejected up front by the dozens of profiles that use the racist phrase "No spice, no rice." Seeing so many people say so openly that they think Latino guys are unattractive hasn't exactly made Jaime feel better about his chances of finding something genuine.

Jaime's shame about going so long without a relationship is precisely what made it harder for him to find a relationship.

This is partly because shame doesn't just feel terrible—it also makes people withdraw, self-isolate, and even avoid entire areas of their lives. Sometimes, this means people avoid going out and trying new things; other times, it means skipping out on great opportunities. And a lot of the time, it leads people to avoid their own family and closest friends too.

All of this avoidance, though, only reinforces the false narratives that shame creates. After all, if you're ashamed because you feel like nobody likes you, avoiding your friends is going to end up making you feel worse. If you're going through a rough patch, but you avoid asking for help because you're ashamed and feel like a failure, your life is probably going to be a lot harder to get back on track.

A lot of people experience shame on a daily basis, though it can be surprisingly hard to detect. Of course, shame feels awful, but there are a lot of emotions that feel awful. It often takes people careful reflection and practice to be able to consistently recognize shame when it comes up.

This is partly because, as psychologist and shame specialist Dr. Jane Bolton writes, shame shows up in many different forms (2009). These are mostly feelings we already know under other names, like shyness or embarrassment. Dr. Bolton divides shame into different types based on what they're about: shyness is shame in the presence of a stranger, discouragement is shame about temporary defeat, embarrassment is shame in front of others, and self-consciousness is shame about performance.

However, there's also another class of shame: chronic shame. According to Dr. Bolton and renowned psychology authors like Brené Brown, chronic shame doesn't just last longer than these temporary shames that we all experience. Chronic shame is also different because of where it comes from: a pervasive belief you are flawed, unlovable, unworthy, or inferior (Brown 2013).

Are any of these forms of shame ones you struggle with? It's important to get used to identifying what the different forms of shame feel like in your body when they crop up. Shame can show up in your body in many different ways, especially with different types of shame like shyness or self-consciousness. In that, it's just like our other emotions: sadness, anger, love, excitement, and more. They all show up in different types and flavors.

For example, when shame crops up for you, you might feel your throat tighten, your hands tingle, or your muscles tensing.

When you're embarrassed, you might feel your face flush or your cheeks burn. If you're feeling shy, you might feel butterflies in your stomach or like you're sinking into the floor. (Or like you *wish* you could sink into the floor.)

You could also feel cold, heat, weakness, shaking, restlessness, numbness, lightness, heaviness, and more, all over your body or only in specific parts.

These bodily sensations can also be more complex and have specific ideas or metaphors attached to them—having "butterflies in your stomach," for example. You might also feel like you've just had the emotional equivalent of a gut punch, feel like other people's gazes are being imprinted on the back of your head, imagine you've suddenly been caught doing something wrong, or want to temporarily disappear.

Everyone experiences shame to some degree, and it's perfectly normal. Shame becomes a problem when it's the product of an underlying sense of inferiority that follows you across different areas of life and makes it harder for you to relate to others. And like many other things in psychology, shame becomes a clinical ("official") problem when it starts causing significant problems for you. This might be when shame makes it painful to spend time with your friends or leads you to avoid your problems instead of asking for the help you need. Take Jaime's feeling that he's somehow abnormal for not having been in a relationship for so long, and the loneliness he feels, from both his sense he's alone in this experience and the feeling he can't be honest with others in his life.

According to the Compass of Shame theory (Nathanson 1997), people who experience chronic shame will often psychologically protect themselves by withdrawing, punishing themselves, attacking others, or inflating their own egos. Here are some questions to get you thinking about shame, inferiority, and wellness, and the places these concepts might have in your life.

AWARENESS EXERCISE

- What are the places or situations where you tend to feel shame?
- What does it feel like in your body when you are overcome with shame? Where in your body do you feel it? Are there different sensations in different parts of your body?
- On a scale of 1–10, how intensely do you generally experience shame when it shows up?
- On a scale of 1–10, how much does your shame get in the way of your overall wellness?
- How do you tend to protect yourself when you start feeling too ashamed?
- How could you protect yourself from intense shame in the future?
- Is there anyone you can turn to for help, comfort, or protection when you're struggling with shame?
- What are a few concrete reasons why you shouldn't feel inferior to other people? You may want to start by thinking of specific people around whom you feel a sense of inferiority and shame, and work backward from there.

SOURCES OF SHAME

As a GBTQ guy, you might've had multiple experiences, from early childhood on, where the seeds of shame were planted. There are a lot of different things that you might have had negative experiences with, including gender norms, disapproving parents, school athletics, not fitting in, bullying, being interested in the arts or other feminized activities, negative or rigid messages in places of worship, and explicit homophobia or transphobia.

And of course, all of those experiences can make you feel even more shame when combined with feeling uncomfortable, diminished, or undeserving due to your race, economic class, disability, or some other facet of your identity.

However long your list of reasons may be, know that all children struggle with shame, and shame truly is possible to heal from.

In your journal, try to identify six of your personal sources of shame. These can be events, experiences, specific interactions, periods in your life, physical settings, or people.

Sit with the memories that these sources of shame evoke, and reflect on them. Create space—whether through journaling, movement, artwork, a creative practice, conversations with friends and loved ones, or any other means—to understand and express the sadness, anger, and grief you might feel.

Also, know that it's likely that you've tried to take responsibility for negative experiences that you had no control over. According to Dr. Margaret Paul, a best-selling psychology author, many people grow attached to using self-blame to feel like they're more in control (2011). You might think things like, "If this"—experiences of being judged, treated as other or less than—"is my fault, then I can be in charge of keeping it from happening again." Does this resonate with you? If yes, write about the experience, or find some other way to process it, like the following Digging Deeper exercise.

DIGGING DEEPER

You still have a relationship to the people, places, and things that planted the seeds of shame for you, even if they're technically far in the past. The same goes for the people, places, and things that make you experience shame in the present day. This may not be a fun way to think about it, but it is a good thing: by exploring those connections, you can explore ways to heal yourself.

And, of course, as you work through these questions, you'll be strengthening your ability to understand and untangle your thoughts, your emotions, and, ultimately, yourself.

So, let's delve into your relationship with shame and your sources of it. Here are some questions to consider:

1. Do you think you carry any shame related to your sexuality, gender, or romantic identity? How do you experience that shame?

2. Do you believe that you carry shame related to your sexual behavior or sexual desires? Where do you think that shame came from?

3. If you had a friend who told you that they were experiencing shame about something similar, what might you tell them?

THOUGHT ANALYSIS: UNREQUITED LOVE

Queer dating pools can feel limited, especially when you've only started exploring relationships. Friendships sometimes hold the dual role of emotional support and potential partnership, blurring the line between friendship and romantic interest. This tendency to fall for a friend may also be heightened by the need to connect with others who understand and affirm one's identity in ways that family or society may not.

You'll find a full copy of this linear process in our online bank at http://www.newharbinger.com/55039.

1. **Situation:** One of my gay best friends is someone I've developed feelings for. We're hanging out and he tells me about someone else he hooked up with.

2. **Feelings and behaviors:** Shame, envy, sadness, inferiority, self-critical, unworthy, invisible, vulnerable. I am visibly sad and less talkative. I begin imagining what it could be like if he and I were together.

3. **Prominent unhelpful thought:** "I'm not as sexually exciting as other guys. If my best friend can't see me, no other guy will."

4. **Evaluate:** I have not had much success at meeting guys or having fun dates. I joked about us dating and he said, "Can you imagine?" and laughed. That said, my bestie has dated other guys that he originally "friend-zoned." Also, I've become friends with a couple of guys post-hookup who actually wanted more, but I chose not to pursue it, so people are interested in me.

5. **Balanced alternative thought:** "Instead of grieving what I'm not getting, I could focus on the friendship I am getting; also, not everyone wants to give up the process of 'looking.'"

DIGGING DEEPER

1. How can you interrupt the thoughts that shame creates for you? Is there a self-talk script you can use or a specific behavior you can do when you're struggling? For example, you might repeat "I am worthy" to yourself or engage in your favorite hobby.

2. How might you "undo" some of the shame you've internalized?

3. If you were to let go of people, places, or things that set off your shame, what would the trade-off be?

THOUGHT ANALYSIS: RACIALIZED STRESS

1. **Situation:** I went to a house party Friday night, and it was mostly white guys. There were three South Asian ("brown") guys total, including me. I saw one of the brown guys being talked to the most.

2. **Feelings and behaviors:** Shame, jealousy, withdrawn, arousal. I began to chat with new guys and distract myself from the thing that was bothering me.

3. **Prominent unhelpful thought:** "It's hard to meet white guys that are into brown guys. Attention from a white guy would mean I'm

particularly attractive. And if that's true, the other brown guy is my competitor."

4. **Evaluate:** I know that I get less attention from white guys when there are many brown guys around. The hierarchy of social and sexual desirability is real; I see it play out online and on dating apps all the time. However, me and the other brown guy know nothing about each other, so a competition is not warranted. And I do get attention from all kinds of people—white or otherwise—in many contexts.

5. **Balanced alternative thoughts:** "Wanting to compete and devalue a fellow brown queer person is my own internalized racism. Frankly, brown guys are in the minority in this space; if white guys are into us, the competition is among *them*. Nevertheless, I need to start working on the ways I devalue myself and 'my people.'"

DIGGING DEEPER

1. Think about shame as a separate entity. Does "the shame" have an objective when it comes to your worth, progress, or ability to move through the world? What purpose might the shame serve?

2. What makes you feel like you're actually on par with others, rather than inferior to them? Are there specific settings, situations, or conditions that make you feel that way?

3. In your experience of shame and its many roots, whom do you most associate it with? Perhaps a teacher, bully, parent, sibling, or peer at school?

THE EMPTY CHAIR: YOUR CHILDHOOD BULLY

Think back to when you were in school. Was there someone who made fun of you? Multiple people? Perhaps the person you're thinking of wasn't quite a bully, but you felt a deep sense of shame in their presence. Identify one person and put them in the empty chair.

This exercise will help you learn how to both talk through and separate yourself from your shame—things that are easier said than done, but very powerful once you start to get the hang of them.

Some of the things you say in this role-play may be things you're talking about for the very first time. If that's the case, I'm proud of you for finally speaking that into the world. Doing so can be powerful.

Your shame and anxiety might very well flare up during this role-play. If it's too painful, please stop and take a breath. You can always return to this later.

I promise that this exercise is worth it, even if it might be hard. Like in the earlier exercises, pick a memory or a person that isn't too overwhelming for you to handle right now. Even though the exercise will probably still be uncomfortable, letting that discomfort surface is one of the first steps toward releasing your shame. After all, you can't release what you keep locked down in the depths of your mind.

Step 1: Create the Space

- Find a quiet and private space where you feel comfortable. Place two chairs facing each other—one chair represents you, and the other represents your childhood bully.
- Take a few deep breaths, grounding yourself in the present moment.

Step 2: Speak to the Bully

- Tell the bully the first thing that comes to mind.
- Here are some prompts: What do you remember about them? How did they make you feel? What impact did their words and actions have on you? What fantasies did you have about confronting or becoming them? What did you wish had happened back in the day (e.g., having a witness, seeking justice, accountability, revenge, tables turned, etc.)?

Step 3: Switch Chairs and Embody the Bully

- Now switch chairs. You're the bully and the empty chair is you—you're both your adult selves talking about the past.

- Tell the empty chair anything that comes to mind. Here are some prompts: Explain why you behaved badly and what turned you into a bully. How you struggled in ways that others couldn't see. How you wished for your own childhood to be different. Perhaps how you paid for your bad behavior later on in life. Why the adult in you is sorry for causing them pain.

Step 4: Conclusion

- After sitting in the bully's chair, return to your original seat.

- Take a moment to reflect on how it felt to confront this person, even if they didn't respond the way you wanted them to.

- Take a deep breath and reground yourself in the present.

REFLECTIONS

Here are some questions you can use to reflect on the exercise and how it felt.

- What was the experience of talking to your childhood bully like for you? Where did it take you back to? What were some of the unexpected details or feelings that showed up?

- Did you find any relief in being able to confront the bully?

- Was there lingering pain?

- How did you feel once you switched chairs and had to speak from the bully's perspective?

- What was your physical and emotional response to the apology?

- Overall, how was this role-play experience for you?

When something is shameful, there's always the temptation—sometimes the unbearably strong temptation—to avoid the thought of it forever. To push it down as far as possible.

It's completely understandable to want to never think of the things that bring you shame. Shame is often incredibly painful, even unbearable, and chronic shame all the more so.

If pushing shame and other negative emotions down like that could work, though a lot of therapists would be out of a job, a lot of people would have a much easier time healing the wounds within themselves. But unfortunately, it doesn't work like that. Suppression and repression are never true healing. They simply leave the shame to fester—sometimes below your conscious awareness, sometimes painfully clear.

Like a physical wound, in order for shame that has festered to truly heal, it must be lanced and drained. It must be brought out into the light.

This exercise is incredibly difficult because it requires you to reflect on painful memories and confront them. It also puts you in a difficult position where you could feel like you're trying to defend someone who attacked you. To clarify: you do *not* need to excuse anyone's bigoted attitudes or behavior. However, getting into the headspace of the perpetrator, possibly generating some empathy for them, might allow you to see them as weaker than you previously imagined. This has the potential to take away some of their power and help you get in touch with the sadness and grief of what they left you with: chronic shame. You shouldn't have to "forgive and forget." On the contrary, it's more helpful to create a goal to "remember, reflect, and release."

I encourage you to sit with your thoughts and emotions as we turn to the next chapter, where we'll discuss an area where shame originates for many people: your family of origin.

Chapter 4

FAMILY AND CULTURE

As a GBTQ guy navigating the complexities of life, your experiences within your family of origin and cultural background play a significant role in shaping your mental health and overall well-being. Let's delve into these elements together, exploring how they might resonate with your personal journey.

AWARENESS EXERCISE

Read the following questions and simply notice what thoughts, images, memories, and feelings come up for you. Go slow.

- When you think about the word "family," who comes to mind? Just hold them in your mind for a moment.
- Think back to a pleasant memory with your family of origin. Where were you physically? Who was around? How old were you?
- Think back to a difficult family-of-origin memory where you felt rejected for your gender expression or emerging sexual identity by a family member, relative, or someone in your community.
- Meditate for a moment on the terms "family of origin" and "chosen family." How do each of these resonate with your experiences and ideas of families?

FAMILIES AND WELLNESS

The term "family of origin" can refer to blood relatives or the people that made up your household as a child. Imagine your family's structure—perhaps you grew up in a single-parent home, within an extended family, in a foster home, or in some other configuration. Throughout your lifespan, these family structures can have evolving impacts. For instance, as a child in an extended family, you might have benefited from a diverse range of viewpoints and emotional support from various relatives. However, as an adolescent coming to terms with a GBTQ identity, you may have faced challenges if your family adhered to rigid gender roles or lacked understanding of GBTQ issues, leading to potential conflicts during crucial developmental stages. These early interactions lay the groundwork for your comfort with emotions, resilience, and capacity for empathy.

Reflect on the parenting styles you were exposed to—it's essential to consider how these styles may have guided your development over time. Authoritative parents who provided a balance of structure and support likely contributed to a sense of self-worth and autonomy that carried into adulthood, helping you navigate societal pressures with confidence. In contrast, permissive parenting might have offered you the freedom to explore your identity, but perhaps left you wishing for more guidance during your formative years. Neglectful parenting, unfortunately, may have led to difficulties in forming a positive self-identity and could lead to challenges in trusting others and forming intimate relationships. Whatever caregiving and parenting style(s) you were raised with has left its imprint on you, shaping how you see yourself and cope with the pressures of society.

Consider the stability of your family life. That constancy, or lack thereof, can profoundly influence your developmental journey. Events like divorce or relocating to new communities can be particularly destabilizing during adolescence, when identity formation is vital. Such changes might have compounded feelings of isolation or rejection. These early experiences of instability could influence your approach to relationships—potentially leading to heightened vigilance about the stability of your personal and professional life. Conversely, successfully navigating such disruptions can foster adaptability and resilience, skills that are advantageous for anyone, but particularly beneficial for GBTQ men, who may face various societal challenges.

Reflect on who, if anyone, struggled with their mental health within your family. From birth to adulthood, the mental health landscape of your family can heavily influence your understanding and management of your own mental health. If such issues were met with openness and support, this likely fostered an environment where you felt safe to discuss and address your own mental health concerns. This supportive background can lead to a healthier adjustment to your GBTQ identity and better psychological outcomes. However, if mental health was a subject hidden in stigma and silence, this may have impeded your ability to seek help or even to acknowledge your own needs. Over time, this environment could contribute to internalized shame and difficulties in processing emotional challenges related to your GBTQ experience.

Your family's socioeconomic status is another element that can have long-term implications. Financial stability during childhood often equates to greater access to mental health resources, extracurricular activities, and educational opportunities, which can foster a sense of self-efficacy and belonging. Conversely, growing up in economic hardship can place a strain on mental health by amplifying daily stressors and limiting access to supportive groups, programs, and services. These early experiences can shape attitudes toward seeking help, perceptions of self-worth, and stress management throughout your life, potentially influencing how you cope with stressors.

The presence of harmony or conflict within your family is also significant. A harmonious family life can provide a strong foundation of support, promoting resilience against the world's discrimination. In contrast, a tumultuous family environment can instill a pattern of stress and conflict management that carries into other relationships, potentially complicating the journey to self-acceptance and comfort with your GBTQ identity.

Last, consider the role of your siblings throughout your lifespan. Supportive siblings can serve as a vital source of companionship and validation, particularly important during adolescence when peer relationships become central to one's social world. They can bolster your resilience against loneliness and contribute to a positive sense of identity. However, sibling rivalry (or worse), particularly if it involves aspects of your GBTQ identity, can lead to a fraught family dynamic and add to the stress of managing a marginalized identity. The quality of these relationships often sets a template for future social interactions and can be a source either of strength or a recurring challenge.

DIGGING DEEPER

1. How might the structure of your family of origin impact your understanding and acceptance of your GBTQ identity? Were there particular moments or family dynamics that either supported or challenged your journey toward self-acceptance?

2. How did any major changes or instabilities within your family during your adolescence affect your emerging GBTQ identity? In what ways

have these experiences shaped your approach to relationships and changes in your adult life?

3. Consider how mental health issues were addressed within your family. How has the openness or stigma around mental health within your family influenced your own mental health management and acceptance of your GBTQ identity?

ETHNICITY, RACE, CULTURE, RELIGION

Your ethnicity and racial identity are integral to your experience as a GBTQ guy. The cultural context in which you grow up and live profoundly influences how you understand and reconcile your multiple identities. In the United States, you may enjoy a level of freedom and legal recognition that provides a stark contrast to other parts of the world, yet you might still grapple with intersecting forms of racism and homophobia, even within the GBTQ community itself. You may also experience differences between urban and rural communities, liberal versus conservative states, or different life contexts: environments that are accepting and welcoming side-by-side with environments that are punitive or leave you feeling on guard and unsafe. These cultural shifts of acceptance and rejection can often be felt in your body and might lead to self-protective behaviors.

In South America, you may find that traditional values and the pervasive influence of the Catholic Church impact your journey in unique ways. The tight-knit family structures common in these cultures can mean that community and familial acceptance weigh heavily on you, potentially suppressing aspects of your identity. Nevertheless, you may have grown up in a family that engaged with religion in a way that was not punitive; you may have had parents and relatives at the forefront of progressive liberation movements.

In the Asian context, the emphasis on family honor and social standing can impose considerable pressure on individuals. Should you live in a place where being GBTQ is not only stigmatized but also criminalized, the struggle for self-acceptance can be a journey fraught with danger and the fear of social ostracization, or worse. Then again, if you are part of the upper echelon of society, your wealth, networks, and mobility might allow you to explore and express your GBTQ identity quite safely.

If you are from East Africa, where punitive laws against homosexuality are widespread, your very existence might feel like an act of defiance. In these environments, the quest for authenticity can mean a daily negotiation between visibility and safety, often requiring a delicate balance to maintain personal well-being. Despite harmful anti-gay and anti-trans laws, some GBTQ folks will experience differences in acceptance based on the cities they live in and the social-activist communities they are able to build.

Religion and spirituality can either affirm or challenge your sense of self. You might seek comfort in your faith, yet find yourself in conflict with its teachings concerning your GBTQ identity. This dissonance can be especially pronounced if you are an immigrant or the child of immigrants, caught between the beliefs ingrained in you by your family and the often more secular or accepting attitudes of a new homeland.

Discrimination or the process of acculturation, too, can weigh on you. As an immigrant or a child of immigrants, you face the dual challenge of adapting to a new culture while also negotiating the place of your GBTQ identity within it. You must navigate not only the general societal attitudes of your new home, but also the expectations of your cultural community, which might hold differing views on GBTQ issues.

Language and communication are your bridges to the world. Misunderstandings or barriers in these areas can deepen feelings of isolation. However, effective communication allows you to be seen, heard, and understood—a vital aspect of your mental health and integral to fostering a sense of belonging.

And, crucially, the support of your community, chosen family, and social networks is indispensable. A network that sees you and embraces every facet of your identity can serve as a defense against adversity, providing strength and sanctuary from the mental health challenges presented by discrimination and rejection. This community support is vital, whether you find it in vibrant urban centers of the United States, hidden safe spaces within conservative regions, or global connections forged in the digital world.

No matter where your journey takes you, each of these factors interplays in defining your experience as a GBTQ guy. They contribute to the narrative of who you are, offer a mirror to your struggles, and importantly, highlight the resilience and community you can build, no matter where you stand in the world.

Digging Deeper

1. How do you navigate the intersection of your ethnic, racial, and cultural identities with your GBTQ identity? Can you identify moments or environments where one aspect of your identity was more accepted or challenged than the other?

2. Reflect on the norms and expectations from your specific cultural and family backgrounds. How have these influenced your journey toward embracing your GBTQ identity?

3. In what ways has your religion or spirituality impacted your relationship with your GBTQ identity? Have you found reconciliation between these aspects of your life, and if so, how?

Case Scenario

Vitor *is a twenty-eight-year-old Latinx genderqueer person born and raised in Toronto, Canada. Vitor outwardly celebrates their Argentinian heritage but struggles at times. Vitor came out to their family as queer at age nineteen, and though there was some disbelief and disappointment from their parents, who longed for grandchildren, neither parent referenced religion as a reason for their child to change. Nevertheless, Vitor was vocal about rejecting their Catholic faith by age twenty-one, which put them at odds with their family. To their family, ethnic culture and Catholicism could not be separated, so Vitor's parents felt personally insulted.*

Vitor kept as much distance from their family as possible. While the emotional cutoff brought relief from the constant battles, it also brought a sense of grief and loss. Vitor had to grieve the idea of the close-knit family they had, acknowledging that the understanding and acceptance they longed for might never come.

Vitor has spent their twenties meeting other queer and trans people to build a sense of community for themselves. They have noticed that they regularly seek dates and sexual encounters with white gay men. In terms of friendships, they feel discomfort when they are around other Latin Americans who have emigrated more recently. Vitor mentions this to their trusted friend Havier, who understands these experiences immediately and calls them "internalized racism."

On hearing this, Vitor realizes that in their family of origin, there was always a subtle preference for lighter skin and a desire to assimilate to Canadian culture by hiding their accents. Vitor's mother would comment on the light or dark skin tones of a bride or newborn baby, and their father practiced speech during the car ride to social gatherings.

Distant from their family of origin and recognizing that they have learned to not like other people who look like them, Vitor finds themselves feeling angry, guilty, ashamed, and fragmented. They are not sure what healing and meaningful growth can look like for them.

REFLECTIONS

- In what ways do you see aspects of your own ethnic, racial, cultural, and religious backgrounds influencing your self-concept and your relationship to your gender and sexuality?

- In what ways do you experience tension between seeking acceptance from your family and maintaining authenticity in your own identity?

- Vitor's story highlights a struggle with a family that might want to accept them to some extent, but would not want to challenge any aspect of their faith or religious community. Have you experienced similar conflicts within your own community, and if so, how have they shaped your identity and way of being in the world?

- Vitor feels grief about the loss of close familial ties. Can you identify any losses you've had to mourn in the process of embracing your full identity? How have these losses transformed your sense of self and community?

- Vitor seeks connections primarily with white gay men, which Havier labels as internalized racism. Are there any biases you may carry toward your own or other ethnic groups? How might these biases influence your relationship choices?

THOUGHT ANALYSIS: FAMILY TRIGGERS

We all have triggers. Triggers can be people, places, events, or other things that activate our nervous systems to alert us to social, emotional, and physical threats. Some people get along really well with their families and can stay balanced and regulated as their healthy adult self. However, it's not uncommon for an adult who lives independently to experience anxiety before an event where they will see their families of origin. Their triggers are body memories from past experiences, which signal a risk of being pulled into an older dynamic, perhaps one that is less healthy or that draws out parts of their angry child self.

The thought analysis below offers one example of how a family trigger might manifest in your thinking and behavior.

1. **Situation:** You're at a family function, and your father comments on how much you've spent on dining out.

2. **Feelings and behaviors:** Frustrated, ashamed, angry, criticized, on edge. Trying to avoid the conversation topic.

3. **Prominent unhelpful thought:** "He is always criticizing me because I'm the outsider—I'm 'the gay one.' I'll never be an adult in my father's eyes. My father prevents me from 'growing up' because of his scrutiny."

4. **Evaluate:** My father's scrutiny of my behavior consistently brings out my angry inner child. However, I'm accepted and appreciated as a healthy adult by my friends and partner. And my father's behavior is his responsibility. I don't need to respond to him the way I do or at all. I also know he's always been anxious about having enough money for the future. Maybe it's not about me at all.

5. **Balanced alternative thoughts:** "My father's scrutiny might be the only way he knows how to interact with me. And his anxiety is his responsibility. It's not necessarily about me or my sexuality. I might regress to the angry child, but he's not intentionally trying to hold me back. I can stay calm and let the conversation move to something else."

If you find it helpful, try doing a thought analysis on a family or culture trigger that you know bothers you. This thought analysis is available online, along with a blank thought record for you to complete, at http://www.newharbinger.com/55039.

Remember, not all experiences that connect you to your origins are triggers. Some of them may be gateways to exploration and self-love. The scenario below explores what this can look like.

Case Scenario

Jon *is twenty-six years old and has lived most of their life disconnected from their Indigenous roots, having been raised in the metropolis of Sydney, Australia, somewhat distant from their ancestral lands. They have battled deep anxiety and depression, feeling like an outsider in their own skin. They came out as queer and Two Spirit in their early adolescence and were readily accepted by their parents.*

Recent activist events related to land rights piqued Jon's interest, and they attended a rally with a friend. During the rally, there was a speech about challenging white supremacy and reclaiming culture. Another organizer shared a brochure with Jon about healing through culture and invited them to attend an upcoming ceremony with an elder. Jon was anxious about attending. They felt embarrassed for not knowing about ceremonies and their own traditions. They were also uncertain about how much their queerness would be affirmed in this cultural community.

Driven by curiosity and a longing for deeper connection, Jon attended the ceremony the following weekend. On the way, Jon realized this community was where their grandfather grew up. Upon arriving, they were warmly welcomed by the elder who had organized the congregation. There was conversation and exploration around storytelling and ways to honor ancestors. To their surprise, there was quite a bit of emphasis on holding stories of valued Two Spirit people in the community. Jon left that ceremony feeling more connected to themselves. As they drove back to the city, they pulled over unexpectedly to release a few tears. These turned into a deep sob. For the first time, Jon felt pride for being both Indigenous and queer. They also felt a deep sense of grief for not being able to access their own culture and community for so much of their life up until this point.

EMPTY CHAIR: YOUR ANCESTOR

We all have ancestors, guardians of our past, architects of our culture. They lived lives we can only imagine, facing challenges and embracing joys just as we do now. Their stories are etched in time, and their spirits echo within us—in our laughter, our tears, and our heartbeats.

Step 1: Create the Space

- Sit in a chair with an empty chair across from you.
- This empty chair is not simply a piece of furniture; it is a portal, a sacred space for a conversation you've long needed but didn't think was possible. Here, invite an ancestor to sit with you.

Step 2: Start the Conversation

Begin by greeting your ancestor, feeling the weight of their presence, and acknowledging the space they hold in this moment. Now, take a deep breath and ask them these questions, one by one, allowing space for their answers to form in your heart:

- Ancestor, how have you seen queer and trans people express themselves in our family's history?
- In times when you or others like me might have felt unseen, how did you find strength and self-acceptance?
- What challenges did you face in your time, and how can I learn from them?
- How can I honor and continue the legacy of queer and trans family members who came before me?
- What words of comfort can you offer me when I feel disconnected from our shared history and heritage?

Step 3: Switch Seats and Speak as Your Ancestor

Now, switch seats. Sit in the ancestor's chair and take a moment to ground yourself in their energy and perspective. As the ancestor, read the following affirming responses aloud, modifying them if or as you like, observing how they resonate with you:

- Throughout our lineage, there have been many like you, each with their own way of being true to themselves. They lived with courage, and so do you.

- In the moments of feeling unseen, I found strength in the love I held for myself and the certainty that my truth was worth embracing.

- My challenges were many. I loved in secret. I tried to be brave in my own way. I was mistreated at times. I felt shame. I was also deeply scared for so many reasons. I envy the language you have to describe yourself. I'm in awe of the opportunities that lie before you that I didn't have. I did find joy in my life. I was undoubtedly resilient. You carry this resilience within you, ready to face anything with grace.

- You honor our legacy simply by being who you are—bravely and authentically. Let your light shine. Don't let anyone erase you (or us!) from the family history. Don't let people tell you that queer and trans experience is not part of our culture or part of our religious histories. We are, and always have been, more than one thing.

- When life feels tough, you might fall into the trap of thinking it's because something is wrong with you or that the world doesn't have a place for you. Remind yourself you're paving a new path. That's hard work. It's also isolating, because you're not sure where you'll end up. I call that queer joy!

Step 4: Conclusion

- Once you feel you have come to a stopping point in the conversation, return to your original seat.

- Take a moment to reflect on how it felt to sit and speak with your ancestor. Breathe deeply and return to the present moment, knowing that your ancestors are carried within you.

Chapter 5

MILESTONE HETERO-NORMATIVITY

In every culture, certain milestones mark progress through life—graduation, moving out of your childhood home, marriage, having children, and more. However, these milestones can feel limiting and marginalizing for those whose identities, relationships, and life journeys deviate from mainstream societal norms. When your achievements and experiences of growth do not align with more widely acknowledged milestones, you can feel like you're not making the right kind of progress in your life, or you might fear that no one appreciates the challenges and strengths required for taking a different path in life.

For queer and trans people who are participating in or observing the milestone celebrations of their heterosexual counterparts, a complex emotional experience can emerge. You might feel joy, shame, envy, or alienation, perhaps all at once. The complexity of these emotions and thoughts is a response to the phenomena of *milestone heteronormativity*. This refers to the societal expectation that certain life milestones—particularly those related to romantic relationships and family planning—are universal markers of progress and success. These are heteronormative milestones, meaning they assume and prioritize heterosexual and cisgender experiences. For individuals whose identities, relationships, and life paths diverge from these mainstream norms, such milestones can feel exclusionary and marginalizing.

Confronting milestone heteronormativity means grappling with the internal conflicts that arise when your growth is rendered invisible and your developmental achievements are undervalued in mainstream culture.

AWARENESS EXERCISE

Reflect on moments when you were celebrating a milestone for a straight, cis counterpart, such as a family member, friend, or colleague.

- What feelings did you experience? How did they mix together?
- Did anything get in the way of your joy for the other person?
- If you imagine that you were the person being celebrated—are there challenges that would make such a celebration different for you?

Two common milestones largely defined by heterosexual culture are weddings and announcing a new child. Consider the following scenario to see if it resonates with you.

Case Scenario

Zach, *a successful Italian American real estate agent in his early forties, loves his life! He's a gay man who is doing well in his professional life and has a full social calendar. He has a supportive and loving family, consisting of four straight siblings who he's always felt have stood by him through "thick and thin." Still, they don't quite understand his world.*

Recently, Zach attended a cousin's wedding and a baby shower for a colleague in the same weekend. He found himself extremely irritable by the end of the weekend. When asked what might have "gotten to him," he recalled a subtle unease at the wedding, where his cousins were all talking about "Who's next?" His cousin Lucy asked him if he'd ever want to get married, and Zach shrugged his shoulders and said, "Maybe. If it's in the cards...who knows!" Part of him wanted to share that he started dating someone a few months ago, but he held back. He considered sharing the bare minimum about the relationship but then got anxious about being expected to introduce this new boyfriend to his family. He was aware that significant intimate partners flow in and out of his life in a way that his family wouldn't quite understand. They'd think he was "just having fun" and "not ready to settle down." He drank a bit more than usual and pushed on through the reception.

While hungover, he made his way to his colleague's baby shower. The familiar unease emerged when he entered the room draped in baby blue and was asked to help arrange the cupcakes—also blue. While opening gifts, the mother-to-be held up a series of sports-themed onesies and said, "I'm so excited to have a little boy. He's going to be a soccer guy like his dad!" Zach recalled his own father wanting him to play ice hockey until he had a meltdown on the ice and begged his mom to get him off the team.

Was it just a busy weekend that drained his social battery, or could there be something deeper going on with Zach?

MILESTONE MEANINGS

If you can see yourself in Zach's experiences, consider more deeply what might bother you about attending a straight wedding or a baby shower as a queer person. There's a chance you may love both events, and yet they may still leave you feeling uneasy. Let's unpack the social and cultural elements that make these experiences challenging.

First, the celebration of someone else's life partnership might highlight your singleness. As a heterosexual union, it's a reminder that the larger world doesn't recognize the landscape of connection-seeking you operate in. In Zach's case, he's experienced a series of short-term relationships that were deeply meaningful. He hopes to have something last longer, but for him, shorter doesn't mean insignificant. That's because the purpose of his relationships isn't to move along the typical escalator: marriage, owning a home, having children, getting a bigger home "for the kids," and then coaching children through another series of milestones. For Zach to challenge the relationship escalator, he likely had to grieve what his life would not look like some time ago, and this celebration of other people's life choices likely activates that grief and alienation. Zach also prioritizes sexual exploration and negotiating nonmonogamy in the context of a long-term relationship—this isn't easy cocktail conversation at most predominantly straight events.

When asked about marrying, Zach reflected on having the legal right to marry but also knowing that arranging and hosting a wedding might not be as easy for him—specifically because he's queer. He's not sure how accepting different relatives might be. Also, he would have to think about how he distinguishes between friends and family for invitations, given that blood relatives aren't always prioritized over chosen family, friends in poly relationships, supportive queer elders, or past intimate relationship partners. There might be an additional concern about ensuring all his guests, including his gender-non-conforming kin, feel comfortable and safe at such a celebration.

It's possible that as a queer person, you have rejected the idea of marriage altogether, yet still feel a wave of mixed feelings while participating in someone else's milestone because you have a tacit awareness of how that exact event would be more challenging for you to achieve if you did want it.

Consider the cultural hoopla around having a child. If you've been to a baby shower, you may have felt discomfort at the distinctly blue or pink decorations as you heard people predict the child's future in gendered terms. As a queer and perhaps trans person, you know very well how harmful these assumptions can be, but you're also aware that saying so would not go over well. You may feel a kind of gut punch if you pause to consider all the praise heterosexual couples get for having visible evidence of condomless sex (after marriage, of course). As a queer guy, you'll likely have encountered people who still equate condomless sex with death or illness among queer men. Condomless sex between straight people is rarely referred to as "risky behavior" and never as "barebacking."

If you want children yourself, you'll know that the process is more expensive and arduous than it is for the average straight couple. If you wanted children at one point but gave up that pursuit because it didn't fit into your world as a queer person, you may experience a revival of grief around that. If you've never wanted children, you may be thinking about what legacy-making means in your life, and perhaps feel sad to know it may not be acknowledged or celebrated as effortlessly as a new baby arriving in a heterosexual family.

These moments of reflection and alienation are your responses to milestone heteronormativity. They can impact your self-worth and disrupt your understanding of achievement. They can contaminate your evaluation of progress and alter how you engage with significant events in the lives of people around you.

Digging Deeper

- How do you engage with milestone heteronormativity in your life? Do you resist it, conform to it, or try not to think about it?

- Try putting into words what you've had to grieve as a result of not being cisgender or heterosexual. Remember, grief is a response to loss, and you can grieve the losses that come from strained relationships, disappointing parents, estrangement from religious communities, or taking a path less traveled.

- How have you come to define progress and success differently than the cisgender and heterosexual people you grew up around?

REDEFINING MILESTONES

Here's a detailed list of milestones that are more specific to the experiences of queer and trans folks. Note the ones that stand out to you.

PSYCHOLOGICAL MILESTONES

- Coming out to yourself
- Unlearning teachings that equate queerness with sin
- Exploring authenticity while challenging gender norms in school or other environments
- Overcoming internalized homophobia, biphobia, or transphobia
- Navigating gender dysphoria and body acceptance
- Developing a positive view of your identity
- Learning to "bounce back" from microaggressions and bullying
- Managing the anticipation of bigotry and rejection
- Educating yourself on sexual health and sexuality

INTERPERSONAL MILESTONES

- Experiencing your first LGBTQ+-inclusive social gathering
- Participating in LGBTQ+-specific events (e.g., Pride, Trans Day of Visibility)

- Coming out to family and friends
- Choosing a new name or new pronouns
- Forming a chosen family and supportive networks
- Navigating relationships with nonaffirming family members
- Building and maintaining romantic relationships in the face of stigma and very little cultural representation
- Experiencing validation of bisexual identity in relationships
- Establishing boundaries with people and settings that are nonaffirming
- Establishing boundaries around misgendering and deadnaming

SOCIAL MILESTONES

- Finding and participating in queer community groups and events
- Engaging in queer advocacy and activism (e.g., volunteering at an HIV service organization)
- Experiencing legal recognition of relationships (e.g., marriage equality)
- Gaining access to queer-affirming healthcare and resources
- Experiencing societal recognition and validation of gender
- Navigating public spaces safely and confidently as a queer or trans person
- Legal recognition of nonbinary gender (e.g., on ID documents)
- Legal changes (e.g., name and gender marker updates)
- Sharing photos and content on social media that makes your queerness more visible

MEDICAL MILESTONES

- Learning to communicate about sexual health with your peers and better with your healthcare professionals
- Accessing LGBTQ+-affirming healthcare providers
- Beginning hormone therapy
- Undergoing gender-affirming surgeries or treatments
- Navigating healthcare systems for partner/spouse recognition (e.g., visitation rights)
- Planning and decision-making for reproductive health (as a trans person or in general)
- Accessing mental health services that understand and support LGBTQ+ issues

Feel free to add more to this list! Once you've identified all the milestones that resonate with your trajectory in life, let's reflect on all the work you put into each of these.

DIGGING DEEPER

- What are some of the physical, emotional, and social risks you've confronted in order to meet the milestones you've identified?
- In what ways have you grieved and grown, or turned isolation into innovation, as you moved through your own milestones?
- What it would mean for you to honor each of these milestones and celebrate them?
- If the heterosexual people and communities you're connected to acknowledged each of your milestones, how might that change how you see yourself?

MILESTONE ACTION PLAN

- Acknowledge that queer lives may follow different trajectories, and these paths are equally valid. Celebrate personal milestones that matter to you, like coming-out anniversaries or significant relationship anniversaries, even if they aren't recognized by society at large.

- Build your own traditions with friends, family, or community that reflect and celebrate your life experiences and values.

- Engage with support groups or online communities that affirm the diversity of experiences in the queer community.

CBT PROBLEM SOLVING

You can always revisit a situation where you've been confronted by difficult feelings of someone else's milestone, consider the automatic thoughts that arise, and then consider more balanced, alternative thoughts that support you. However, it may be best to look forward and do some anticipatory problem solving. At some point, you are going to get triggered by milestone heteronormativity. It is unavoidable. Let's use Zach's example to see what CBT problem solving might look like.

- **Situation:** Cousin asks, "Do you think you'd want to get married some day?"

- **Feelings:** Anxious, alienated, hopeful, confused, overwhelmed.

- **Thoughts:** I want to say "no" but don't want to explain myself. I could say "yes" but won't be able to really talk about my thoughts on marriage and resisting the relationship escalator.

- **Problem:** I feel emotionally triggered, and I'm unsure of how to bring my queer self into the conversation.

- **Goal:** To participate authentically without seeming righteous or having to overexplain myself.

- **Possible solutions:** I could give any answer (yes/no/maybe) followed by a light-hearted response (e.g., "Yes, but with more glitter involved!"

"Nah, in this economy?"). Or I could make a succinct statement that acts as a subtle invitation for more conversation (e.g., "I've been thinking about whether or not marriage would actually change my relationship").

- **Evaluate solutions:** Using humor keeps it short while conveying a subtle critique. An indirect invitation to a deeper conversation could make me (and perhaps the other person) feel more seen.

- **Plan of action:** Now that I have two thought-out options in mind, I can decide on which route to go in the moment.

Now, identify a situation where you'll be confronted with milestone heteronormativity, use this problem-solving template to consider your thoughts and feelings, convert those into a goal for the interaction, and then identify possible solutions.

THE EMPTY CHAIR: COMPARISON STICK

In this exercise, we will focus on your "comparison stick," a mechanism that is central to your emotional response to milestone heteronormativity. Again, milestone heteronormativity refers to the heteronormative societal expectations and pressures around achieving certain life milestones—such as marriage, having children, or career success. This exercise is designed to help you explore the internalized pressures and expectations you may have around life milestones, particularly those influenced by heteronormative standards.

Step 1: Create the Space

- Please take a seat and ensure you are comfortable.
- Imagine that in the empty chair across from you sits the person or the societal voice that represents the expectations and pressures you feel around life milestones.

Step 2: Speak to the Comparison Stick

- Begin by addressing the person or voice in the empty chair. You can start with something like, "Hello, comparison stick. You represent the pressures and expectations I feel about... [mention specific milestones]."

- Now, speak to your comparison stick about how these expectations affect you. What feelings arise when you think about these milestones? How do these pressures influence your decisions and self-perception?

Step 3: Switch Chairs and Embody the Comparison Stick

- Switch places and sit in the empty chair.
- Respond as if you are the comparison stick. Explain why and how you began to collect the signs of progress and comparison from your environment.
- Describe how these expectations came to be important in your life and what they signified to those around you.
- Acknowledge that you have been trained by society to assume your milestones are shared by everyone, and that assumption leaves people out.

Step 4: Conclusion

- Switch back. Take a deep breath.
- Express gratitude to the comparison stick for trying to be helpful and help you fit in.
- Then, share what your actual milestones have been.
- Make an agreement with the comparison stick that you will both try not to convert others' experiences of growth into personal criticism.

Chapter 6

DISENFRANCHISED GRIEF

Most people are familiar with the idea of grief as loss resulting from death of a loved one or an important figure. Before we discuss disenfranchised grief, it's important to consider some common terminology around grief and loss:

- **Loss** is the absence of a person, place, time, opportunity, experience, self-concept, conceptual understanding, plan, or dream that is personally significant.

- **Grief** is the emotional response to loss; it also encompasses the personal and collective meanings given to the loss.

- In the context of death-related losses, *bereavement* is a mental headspace we enter following a significant loss, and *mourning* is usually a culturally sanctioned time period for adapting to a loss.

However, the concept of grief goes far beyond death and dying. We experience non-death losses regularly. These can range from the end of a relationship or school program to unfulfilled dreams. You might recall your own experiences during the COVID-19 lockdowns. You were likely experiencing *anticipatory and ambiguous grief*—predictable but uncertain losses around socializing, community connection, human touch, milestone and seasonal events, and potential loss of vulnerable family members.

You've also likely observed that not all forms of grief are acknowledged equally. According to Kenneth Doka, *disenfranchised grief* is "grief that results when a person experiences a significant loss and the resultant grief is not openly acknowledged, socially validated, or publicly mourned. In short, although the individual is experiencing a grief reaction, there is no social recognition that the person has a right to grieve or a claim for social sympathy or support" (2008).

Doka suggests disenfranchised grief occurs for a number of reasons that usually fall into one (or more) of the following categories:

- The loss isn't seen as worthy of grief, such as with the death of a pet or perhaps non-death losses like loss of employment.
- The relationship is stigmatized, such as the loss of a partner in an extramarital affair or an incarcerated family member.
- The mechanism of death is stigmatized, such as death by suicide or drug overdose.
- The person grieving is not recognized as a griever, such as coworkers or ex-partners, or loss due to war as experienced in a diasporic community.
- The way someone is grieving is stigmatized, such as leaning into drug or alcohol use, or the absence of an outward grief response as expected by others.

AWARENESS EXERCISE

1. Reflect on an experience of loss where your grief was socially and culturally acknowledged. How did you know you could grieve outwardly? What were the conversations and immediate responses to your loss?

2. Now reflect on an experience of loss where your grief was disenfranchised. What made you feel like grieving outwardly wasn't going to be well understood? Who do you wish could have been a witness to your loss, when in reality, they couldn't appreciate that you were grieving?

QUEERING DISENFRANCHISED GRIEF

Let's explore the types of losses specific to GBTQ communities that might result in disenfranchised grief. Along the way, you are invited to reflect on whether these experience resonate with you personally, and also consider how collective losses can continue to reverberate in your mind and your community. Take time to use the questions that follow each example to dig deeper and make use of the exercises for brief grief work.

LONG-TERM SURVIVOR'S GUILT

During the height of the AIDS epidemic in the US, AIDS killed over 324,000 people between 1987 and 1998. The crisis decimated a generation of gay men, baby boomers born between 1951–1970, aged 25–44 at the time (Rosenfeld 2018). Queer communities grieved individual and collective losses. Older gay men living with HIV who survived the epidemic are long-term survivors. Surviving when others have passed can anchor a heavy guilt in the soul. It is the guilt of breathing when breath has been denied to loved ones; the guilt of continuing life's journey with a companion forever halted midstride.

Consider John, who knows this burden intimately. At seventy, he is a product of survival and loss, having lived through the peak of the AIDS epidemic. His partner was one of its many casualties, leaving John in the throes of survivor's guilt. This grief is disenfranchised, as society's collective memory often fails to keep pace with individual mourning, leaving survivors like John in an unacknowledged space where their profound losses are not granted the full attention they deserve.

BRIEF GRIEF WORK

Survivor's guilt often arises from the intense emotional pain of having lived through a traumatic event that others did not survive. This type of guilt is particularly potent among long-term survivors of the AIDS epidemic, who carry the burden of outliving their peers. Survivors may feel undeserving of their survival, haunted by questions of why they lived while others did not. This emotional struggle can challenge their sense of safety, trust, and self-worth (Pearlman et al. 2014).

In the book *Treating Traumatic Bereavement: A Practitioner's Guide*, the authors suggest reframing the narrative, which involves shifting your perspective to recognize and emphasize the positive impacts you have had on others and your community (Pearlman et al. 2014). This exercise helps in transforming feelings of guilt into a sense of purpose and gratitude.

Steps:

1. Identify specific moments when you have felt survivor's guilt. Write these instances down in detail. Include the thoughts, feelings, and physical sensations you experienced.

2. For each instance, consider the impact you've had on others and your community since surviving the epidemic. Think about the support, love, and guidance you've offered to friends, family, and fellow community members.

3. Reframe your narrative by writing down your contributions and impact; include statements that reaffirm your purpose and highlight your gratitude for opportunities that survival has given you.

DIGGING DEEPER

1. If you're a long-term survivor or were present during the height of the epidemic, how has the grief manifested in your life? What has supported you in your grief and in growing around your grief?

2. Regardless of your age and historical reference point, in what contexts have you experienced a kind of survivor's guilt? What does it look like to counter the feelings of guilt?

3. Whether you're younger or older, what is the value of intergenerational friendships (or what might it be) with other queer men in your life? If you've not been able to cultivate these types of connections, what might be needed to allow them to flourish?

LOSS OF CULTURAL CONNECTION

Many queer and trans guys leave their countries of origin seeking a more accepting climate for gender and sexual minorities. This migration pattern can take the form of international schooling, expatriate employment opportunities, or asylum seeking. However, when guys arrive in what's supposed to be a safe haven, they often experience grief and loss of cultural connection with their country of origin. Even in multicultural cities, white gay men are often overrepresented in mainstream queer spaces.

A loss of culture can also be experienced by older gay men who are nostalgic for the in-person connection, collective activism, strong bar culture, and community gatherings that have changed shape completely since the rise of digital platforms and online dating apps. With the widespread use of HIV prevention and treatment technologies, there is also a loss of cultural practices that included communication and conversations about sexual health and well-being.

In many ways, the queer immigrant and the queer elder are both custodians of grief for a community and cultural lineage, displaced by development and progress that often does not acknowledge the cost of its advance.

DIGGING DEEPER

1. Have you felt like you've had to choose between a cultural identity and your sexual/gender identity? If you've had to prioritize only one layer of your identity (for reasons of safety, migration, or resistance), how do you experience loss around the other parts of you?

2. Research shows that nostalgia can be positive for well-being, but it can also make people feel stuck (Cheung et al. 2017). What about your nostalgia? How is it keeping part of you alive, feeling connected? Does it facilitate dreaming and optimism for a better world?

BRIEF GRIEF WORK

Traumatic experiences, such as sudden and unexpected losses, can shatter what psychologists refer to as the "assumptive world"—the basic beliefs and understandings we hold about ourselves, others, and the world around us (Pearlman et al. 2014). This concept highlights how trauma disrupts our sense of safety, trust, control, esteem, and intimacy. When these fundamental beliefs are violated, survivors often struggle with intense fears, difficulties in trusting others, and challenges in finding meaning and purpose in their lives.

One way to help is to engage with personal rituals that blend elements from an earlier time (e.g., cultural heritage, younger age) with your current identity to bridge your past and present (Pearlman et al. 2014). These rituals can provide a sense of continuity and belonging, helping integrate your experiences and foster healing. Here's what this can look like:

Steps:

1. Identify elements from an earlier time/place that are meaningful to you (e.g., films, food, storytelling).

2. Connect with your present self and the more recent traditions and practices you've engaged with. Finding people similar to you in some way may be important (e.g., similar cultural background, age, shared history).

3. Create a personal ritual by deciding which elements of the past you might want to combine with the present (e.g., gatherings, getting coffee).

4. Clarify the purpose for the ritual (e.g., to maintain a connection with your cultural roots while building new relationships, to honor the past while adapting to the present).

5. Practice the ritual and return to adjust it when needed.

LOSS OF RELIGION

Loss of a religious community is traumatic. It involves losing relationships, losing access to spaces, and grappling with messages of shame and unworthiness. It can leave you feeling angry, isolated, and directionless. This is what religious trauma and grief can look like.

If you were raised in a religious community, then you know that religion isn't just about God or prayer. It's about community, mutual support, congregation, sermons, teachings, storytelling, customs, gendered expectations, places of worship, yearly observances, rituals, commemorations, culture, devotion, conviction, hierarchies of esteemed and elevated people, and spiritual practice. It's an insular world with a prescribed way of life. While some queer and trans people do not experience conflict between their queer and religious identities, many more have a complicated relationship with religious communities and practices, which have been used to harm them in some way.

Regardless of your current religious views and affiliation, you've likely asked yourself, "Will my religion welcome me or reject me if they know I'm queer or trans?" This question speaks to the anticipatory grief you experienced at a young age. Afterward, you may have found space in your existing religious community, sought a more affirming community, altered your practice and approach to spirituality, or rejected religion altogether. When you find that you don't fit into what you once experienced as "a way of life," you're experiencing deep loss—regardless of whether you left by choice.

DIGGING DEEPER

1. In what ways have you experienced grief and loss related to your experiences, beliefs, and practices of religion? What tends to activate this grief now?

2. When religious groups attack queer and trans people, what feelings and memories does it evoke for you?

3. Conversely, when religious groups are politically attacked, how does this complicate your relationship with that community? Is your intersectional grief acknowledged (e.g., a person is queer and "culturally Muslim"—i.e., not as theologically invested—and they witness and experience Islamophobia constantly. Neither the mainstream queer nor Muslim communities can fully appreciate their grief.)?

BRIEF GRIEF WORK

Religious trauma is painful and can linger for years. It may actually be a less disenfranchised form of grief if you are able to meet and talk with other queer and trans people with similar experiences. However, if you're left grappling with this grief on your own, you can try the following exercise.

Consider Terence, an Irish American twenty-eight-year-old man who feels deep anger and pain toward his Catholic religion. When he came out as bisexual, his parents used their religious beliefs to reject and shame him. This experience led Terence to close the door on all forms of religion, carrying unresolved anger and grief. Recently, Terence attended a Pride parade and saw a float of people who claimed to be both Catholic and queer. This sight triggered intense emotions, causing old wounds to resurface.

Terence wants to prevent having unexpected responses like he did at the parade. Here's what he can try:

Steps:

1. Create a list of physical sites and objects that cause distress, including buildings, posters, online images, churches, etc.

2. Starting with the least distressing thing on the list, Terence should make a plan to be in the presence of the distressing site or object in a way that allows him maximum personal control (i.e., walking by a church alone, viewing an old photo in a private space, etc.).

3. When exposed to the distress, Terence can simply allow himself to feel the mix of emotions that arise. He's encouraged to breathe deeply, reflect, and cry if he needs to. He can stop this exercise at any time.

4. It would be useful for Terence to also journal about the experience and include all cognitive and sensory details (i.e., what he saw, heard, felt, and thought during this experience).

5. Terence should revisit the distressing site or object several days later to see if the intensity of his response has decreased. If so, he may choose to repeat the exercise—or not. If his response is the same, he can create a ritual of confronting these things periodically to see what emerges.

6. Finally, Terence should acknowledge that he has likely developed all-or-nothing thinking as a result of trauma. At this stage, he can spend some time thinking about whether he wants to have a future relationship with the religious community and whether he needs anything further to feel assured that the past is behind him.

NEURODIVERGENCE AND LOSS

Neurodivergence refers to the range of differences in individual brain function and behavioral traits, often encompassing diagnoses and labels such as autism, ADHD, and others. For many, the experience of being neurodivergent intersects with queerness, as both identities can lead to questioning and defying societal norms about gender and sexuality (Rakshit 2023). Discovering the label and receiving a formal diagnosis of neurodivergence later in life can activate a profound sense of grief over the lost time, opportunities, and experiences that might have been different with earlier awareness and understanding. This grief often stems from realizing how long you've been navigating the world without the tools and community that recognition and diagnosis can offer.

For Kgosi, grief manifests through a series of "what-ifs." Diagnosed with ADHD during the COVID-19 pandemic, Kgosi now reevaluates his past struggles. What if he had been diagnosed earlier—would he have understood his academic struggles differently? And if his friends had been more aware of neurodivergence and its ties to queer identity, would they have offered more support, letting Kgosi feel comfortable enough to come out? In truth, the world around him is unlikely to fully recognize the overlapping layers of his internal journey. Nevertheless, Kgosi has been able to grieve and reconceive his narrative as one not of deficit, but of complexity and resilience.

Digging Deeper

- Consider the intersections of your queer and neurodivergent identities, if applicable. How do these aspects of who you are interact to shape your experiences and perceptions of the world?

- In what ways might your understanding of yourself have changed if you had discovered your neurodivergence earlier? What about your relationships, educational or career paths, and self-acceptance?

- Reflecting on "what-ifs" due to delayed diagnosis or recognition of neurodivergence/queerness, what specific experiences or opportunities do you grieve the most?

BRIEF GRIEF WORK

Late diagnoses in neurodivergence can often result in a sense of "lost time" toward personal development and mental health. For some, their experience of personal grief relates to past traumas and mental health struggles that went unaddressed for years (Krouse 2023). This narrative links the delayed resolution of these issues to a prolonged period of mourning over lost time, which could have been mitigated with earlier intervention.

To help you process the grief of lost time more directly, you can create a grief timeline.

Steps:

1. Map out the key moments in your life where the lack of a diagnosis or misinterpretations of your neurodivergent traits led to significant challenges or losses.

2. Next to each, note how you eventually overcame or adapted, focusing on the resilience shown in each situation.

3. Remind yourself that though a balanced view that includes your resilience is always helpful, you're always allowed to experience sadness around loss.

GRIEF AND MASCULINITY

Navigating traditional masculinity often poses unique challenges. The expectations placed upon men to be stoic can be restrictive and damaging, particularly during times of grief. Conventional masculine traits—like suppressing emotions and maintaining an aura of toughness—can conflict with the emotional openness necessary for healthy grieving. These traditional norms can limit your ability to process and express grief effectively, potentially leading to poorer mental health outcomes (Morris 2020). If you've ever felt pressured to appear strong and composed during emotionally turbulent times, such as the illness of a loved one, you're not alone. This pressure is a common experience and can hinder your ability to seek support and express vulnerability, complicating your grief process (Johnson 2023).

As a GBTQ guy, these challenges may resonate deeply due to the additional layers of stigma and expectations related to your sexual and gender identity. The restrictive definitions of what it means to be a "man" can feel particularly constraining. Here are two snapshots of what this can look like:

Ebrahim, *a twenty-six-year-old Bangladeshi British gay man, battles anxiety and self-doubt daily, especially when he's with his family of origin and at gay bars. In both settings, he feels that his masculinity is being scrutinized. Recently, his aunt suggested it's important that Ebrahim get married and have kids to carry on the family name. When he felt annoyed with that conversation, he turned on a dating app, where he was bombarded with ads for pills to enlarge penis size and profiles that said "masc guys only."*

Hiroki, *a thirty-eight-year-old Japanese American trans man, recently lost his father to cancer, which has plunged Hiroki into the depths of grief. As memories of his father surface, he experiences waves of loss, along with the realization of the weight of expectations he bore as his parents' son. These expectations, anchored in the cultural norms of his heritage, underscored the shame and sorrow Hiroki felt as he endeavored to live authentically amid traditional gender dictates. He feels terribly sad that his father has passed but simultaneously feels some relief. While his dad was alive, Hiroki was grieving his gender.*

DIGGING DEEPER

1. How might the concept of "failing gender" have impacted your personal wellness and self-perception? Reflect on instances where you felt you did not meet traditional gender expectations and how this has influenced your emotional and physical health.

2. In what ways have you experienced grief related to your identity from a young age, and how has this manifested in behaviors such as withdrawal, depression, resentment, envy, or grandiosity?

3. Considering the emphasis on physical appearance, like sculpted bodies, among gay men, how might this emphasis be possibly a symptom of grief or coping mechanism for deeper emotional pain?

BRIEF GRIEF WORK

Your grief around gender and masculinity will likely to continue being activated across your life. That doesn't mean you haven't found progress. Rather, it's a new opportunity to rethink the blueprint you've been given (which many people around you still rely on). Create three to five affirmations related to your gender. You know best what your relationship to gender looks like and what affirmations might be most poignant for you. Use the affirmations below to guide you.

- GBTQ guys who make me feel bad about my masculinity are not helpful for my growth. If I want to maintain contact with them, it's most useful to understand their rigidity as a symptom of their own grief.
- I have been socialized as a man in a world where men are told to repress emotion. If I want my masculinity to be more expansive, I can set an intention and goal to build more emotion skills.
- I am more than the expectations placed upon me. My worth is not measured by my adherence to traditional roles, but by the integrity and kindness with which I lead my life.

LOSS RELATED TO DRUG USE

Chemsex, commonly known as "party n' play" (PnP), refers to the use of drugs like crystal methamphetamine, GHB, and mephedrone among GBTQ men to enhance sexual pleasure and endurance, and to lower inhibitions during sexual encounters. GBTQ men are up to twenty times more likely than the general population to engage in chemsex (McGuire et al. 2020).

GBTQ guys often engage in chemsex for reasons that include the desire for increased sexual pleasure and enhanced social connections, as well as a coping mechanism for stigma or stress related to their queer identities. The use of these substances is linked to a heightened sense of community and belonging within certain social circles, despite their potential health risks (Card et al. 2019; McGuire et al. 2020).

Drug-related deaths within the GBTQ community lend themselves to experiences of disenfranchised grief. Stigma around both drug use and queerness marginalizes the grief experienced by partners, friends, and other loved ones.

BRIEF GRIEF WORK

The grief work around drug-related deaths is two-fold: it involves both education and creating space for mourning. If you have not directly been affected by a loss of this nature, education is critical so that others' grief can become more readily acknowledged (and less likely to be disenfranchised). Treat the following statements as truths, and do some personal online research to understand what makes them true and valid. Then, have a conversation with a trusted friend to share what you've learned, along with things you still feel uncertain about.

- People who use drugs care about their own lives and well-being.
- People don't necessarily die from drug overdoses but rather from ineffective drug policies.
- People who use drugs (whether legal or illicit) have a right to harm reduction information and supplies.
- Criminalizing drugs harms people who use them and the communities they live in.
- Drug use is not synonymous with addiction; substance use disorders can be more of an illness for some people rather than a series of choices.
- Chemical dependency can develop over time as someone's life circumstances and relationship with substances evolve.

Now, if you've been directly affected by loss related to drug use, write a brief letter to one specific person (or multiple people) you've lost. Use the following prompts:

- "When I think of you, my mind always goes back to…"
- "To me, your presence was…"
- "I know you faced many battles with…"
- "Knowing that you used substances to facilitate connection is heavy because I'm left thinking about how to stay connected to you and your memory, us and our memories…"

- "We left some things unfinished. I want to tell you… And, I wish we could have talked more about…"
- "I want to say farewell to you, but I suspect you'll show up in my mind when…"

Remember, processing grief is never a singular task. Rather, we learn to live with and grow around grief. If your grief has been disenfranchised, you would not have had much opportunity to honor it. For GBTQ guys, we need to first see our grief as legitimate and then allow ourselves to begin working through it with the objectives of increased resolve, a less fragmented sense of self, and personal growth.

Part 2

YOUR CONNECTIONS

Chapter 7

SEEKING CONNECTIONS

If you've experienced grief in the past, it's because you have allowed yourself to feel love and connection. Connection—whether fleeting or long term—occupies a central role in our lives, especially for GBTQ men. As we navigate through the mesh of dating apps and hookup culture, these platforms offer both unprecedented connectivity and unique emotional landscapes. From the desire for romantic engagement to casual conquests, app culture embodies a modern paradox: an offer of intimacy with the potential for isolation.

MIXED MESSAGES

As a GBTQ guy, you might find that mainstream heterosexual culture often conflates the concepts of long-term relationships (LTRs), commitment, and monogamy. This dominant culture also portrays LTRs as the ultimate goal, idealizing monogamy as a sign of maturity, a natural life stage, and a way to suppress any possible attraction to others. Popular films and TV shows frequently depict a narrative where characters engage in casual sex only until they find "the one" to settle down with—think of romantic comedies where the protagonist's multiple flings are just humorous detours on their journey to true love.

Messages within GBTQ men's culture can be quite different. Here, casual sex might not only be seen as common, but actually celebrated as liberation and an integral part of community identity. The freedom to explore one's sexuality without commitment is often emphasized, and LTRs might be portrayed as less common or organized, with nonmonogamy as a central assumption of the partnership.

These mixed messages can create internal conflicts and confusion about what you should value or pursue. It's okay to feel uncertain or find your path diverging from these scripts. Each person's experiences and desires are unique, and finding a balance that feels right for you—whether it's embracing casual encounters, seeking a long-term partnership, or both—can be a deeply personal journey. Remember, your worth and the validity of your relationships are defined not by these external scripts, but by what makes you feel fulfilled and respected.

DIGGING DEEPER

1. How do the conflicting cultural messages about sex and relationships impact your view and pursuit of intimacy?

2. Reflect on a time when external opinions (or fear of judgment) influenced how you felt about a sexual encounter. How did you feel? If you experienced guilt or shame, how did you make sense of it at the time?

3. If GBTQ culture values both LTRs and casual sex, how does navigating this landscape of connection-seeking affect you emotionally?

REWARDS AND CHALLENGES

So, you're in it. You're embedded in a GBTQ subculture that might have values and perspectives unlike the ones you grew up around. You may not want to pursue multiple forms of romantic and sexual connection, or any for that matter. Nevertheless, the subculture of GBTQ men is often built on the idea that social and emotional rewards come with redefining connection and relationship structures.

While the pursuit of LTRs and casual connections can be rewarding—offering intimacy, validation, and pleasure—it is not without challenges. The fleeting highs of new encounters often come with the lows of ghosting and the struggle of navigating expectations through a screen. Apps, while facilitating connections, can also amplify insecurities about body image and personal worth. LTRs can feel limiting or quickly lead GBTQ guys into grief over their single lives, which once represented independence, autonomy, and a queer way of being. Guys in LTRs who want to negotiate nonmonogamy are also confronted with the challenge of never being taught the skills to do this effectively. For example, some advocates of ethical nonmonogamy will frame jealousy as an individual problem, while others will encourage couples to talk about jealousy and work on discerning when the jealousy conversation is helpful.

EXERCISE: REWARDS AND CHALLENGES

Consider a recent dating or hookup experience. What were the rewards? What challenges did you face? How did you feel about the experience, and what might you change about a future encounter to increase the rewards and limit the less desirable elements? Here are some examples:

- Rewards: self-esteem boost, pleasure and touch, thrills of seduction and cruising, necessary validation (from a variety of sources), sexual exploration and evolution, and a sense of belonging
- Challenges: managing expectations about chemistry, navigating unspoken norms, sitting with rejection, increased body consciousness, app culture that reinforces limited emotional expression, experiences of rejection (including HIV-phobia, racism, and femmephobia)

RELATIONSHIP ORIENTATION

GBTQ subcultures often see nonmonogamy as a normative relationship structure. However, few of us are actually given the opportunity to reflect on the question, "What is your relationship orientation, and how fluid is it?" You likely see your sexual orientation as relatively fixed. In the same way, your tendency to gravitate toward monogamy or nonmonogamy might be similarly seen as a kind of orientation. If this is the case, you'll need a way to communicate about this while dating and pursuing relationships.

Does your relationship orientation lean more toward monogamy or nonmonogamy? Do you find that you appreciate and enjoy high or low emotional exclusivity with a partner? Do you find that you appreciate and enjoy high or low sexual exclusivity with a partner?

Before you're ready to identify your relationship orientation, it's crucial to question the myths surrounding these models and explore what genuinely resonates with your personal needs and values. By understanding your relationship orientation, you can better navigate the complex landscape of modern love.

EXERCISE: MYTHS

The following statements represent myths for different relationship models. Review each one, and do an online deep dive to help you refute each one and gain more perspective on the arguments people make as they attempt to unravel the messages our cultures have taught us.

Monogamy Mythbusting

1. Monogamy is *not* natural for all humans.
2. Monogamy does *not* guarantee emotional security.
3. If you love someone, you *might still* be attracted to other people.
4. Monogamy does *not* inherently mean your relationship is successful.
5. Monogamy is *not* inherently easier than nonmonogamy.

Nonmonogamy Mythbusting

1. Nonmonogamy is *not* all about having a lot of sex.
2. Nonmonogamy *does* involve real commitment.
3. Nonmonogamy does *not* mean at least one person is dissatisfied in the relationship.
4. Nonmonogamy does *not* mean you don't have to deal with jealousy.
5. Nonmonogamy is *not* inherently the reason people's relationships fail.

CBT PROBLEM SOLVING

Imagine you're on a date and the person you've met reveals a relationship orientation that starkly differs from yours. Let's use the CBT problem-solving method to sort through your thoughts and feelings, evaluate your objectives, and consider your options.

- **Situation:** I'm on a date with Jeremy, who is so handsome, but he says his relationship orientation leans toward monogamy, which is different from mine.

- **Feelings:** Anxious, frustrated, sad, slightly righteous.

- **Thoughts:** I doubt Jeremy has tried nonmonogamy. He's probably judging me or thinks I'm not interested in commitment. I hate that he might write me off for this difference!

- **Problem:** We have different relationship orientations.

- **Goal:** Enjoy my time with this attractive human and see if we're into each other.

- **Possible solutions / Evaluations:**

    a. I can ask him if he's been in a nonmonogamous relationship. / This might sound condescending or like I think I know better, which could put him off.

    b. I can ask how he arrived at his relationship orientation and share how I arrived at mine. / This would be less aggressive—and meshes with my agenda for how we might get to know each other.

    c. Share that I see myself as nonmonogamous but would love to have more conversations about this if Jeremy wants. / This is less defensive on my part and more of an invite; it doesn't suggest anything is a dealbreaker at this stage.

    d. I could directly ask if Jeremy would consider being with a non-monogamous person. / This conveys urgency on my part to gain some understanding and certainty about what our future can look like; it could also suggest that there's no point in continuing this date if we're not a match.

- **Plan of action:** Share that I see myself as nonmonogamous but would love to have more conversations about this if Jeremy wants. Additionally, remind myself that my goal is to enjoy my time with Jeremy without deciding whether a future is possible right away. If immediate compatibility and long-term planning were my goals, I could have asked about relationship orientation before we met in person.

GYMNASTICS OF DATING

GBTQ guys usually have a variety of opinions around the timing of sex. Jumping into physical intimacy quickly is not inherently a problem, but it's crucial to check in with your own comfort. You might feel like having sex "too early" clouds your judgment or that it can turn what might be a meaningful connection into something fleeting—or you might feel like emotional and sexual energies are meant to evolve concurrently and intertwine.

When there's a clear sense of mutual interest between you and a partner, you may begin thinking about how to define the relationship. The label "boyfriend" can carry a lot of weight. It often signifies a level of commitment and exclusivity that can be comforting, acknowledging the importance of your relationship. However, this label can also introduce expectations about dates and sleepovers, leisure time, and levels of communication and exclusivity. For those who cherish freedom and flexibility, avoiding labels can reduce pressure and create space to explore the relationship more freely. On the other hand, for those who seek security and reassurance, labels might be important and comforting.

Awareness of your attachment style—whether you tend toward anxiety and fear of losing the other person, or tend toward avoidance and fear of losing yourself—can greatly influence your dating experiences. If you have an anxious attachment style, you might find yourself needing more reassurance and fearing rejection. You may need to communicate openly about your needs, but try to give your partner space to grow into the relationship naturally without feeling pressured. If you lean toward an avoidant attachment style, acknowledging your tendency to pull away and understanding your partner's need for closeness can help mitigate misunderstandings. Recognizing these patterns can lead to a more fulfilling relationship for both partners.

Digging Deeper

1. Think back to a recent date that felt significant. What emotions did you feel during and after the date? What do you think these emotions tell you about what you need or want in a relationship?

2. How do you typically react when someone shows interest in you or when you feel rejected? Do these reactions affect how you approach new relationships?

3. When you meet someone new, how do fear and excitement influence your view of them? Do these feelings change the way you act in the relationship?

4. Recall a time when you decided to define or not define a relationship. What led to that decision, and how did you feel afterward?

5. When you imagine your ideal relationship, what does it look like? How do these thoughts reflect what you deeply value or fear about being close to someone?

EMBRACING INNOVATION

In the landscape of romance, love, sex, and connection, embracing innovation means acknowledging and valuing your journey—whether you are single, exploring multiple relationships, or somewhere else in your journey. It can be useful to remind yourself that while GBTQ guys have a subculture that emphasizes and prioritizes different relationship models than the mainstream heterosexual culture, none of us are handed a guidebook. What we're all embarking on is innovation in our relationships!

Here are some affirming ways to embrace this innovation:

1. **Celebrate your singleness:** If you're currently single, it's a time rich with potential for self-discovery and for setting your own rules in the

dating game. Being single isn't a pause on happiness; it's an opportunity to understand your desires and boundaries without compromise. It's a chance to build resilience and a strong sense of self that you can bring into future relationships, or simply enjoy in your own company.

2. **Redefine long-term relationships:** You may cherish or question the value of long-term relationships. Remember that LTRs don't need to conform to traditional expectations. You get to define what commitment looks like for you—whether that's exclusivity, openness, or even platonic partnerships that defy conventional labels but fulfill your emotional needs.

3. **Explore various forms of connection:** The connections you seek and maintain—romantic, sexual, platonic, or otherwise—are all valid expressions of your need for intimacy. Whether you find that intimacy in the depth of late-night conversations with friends, the fun of casual encounters, or the comfort of a domestic partnership, each form of connection brings its own set of rewarding experiences and challenges.

4. **Confront mixed messages:** You have already received mixed messages about how relationships "should" work. Your innovative approach to these messages—filtering them, adjusting them, or outright rejecting them—is a profound act of self-respect and assertiveness in the face of societal expectations.

Finally, try not to lose yourself in the process of exploration. You bring a unique perspective to how you manage your personal and intimate connections, guided by both desire and a deep understanding of what works best for you. Embracing innovation isn't just about accepting the status quo of your relationship dynamics; it's about actively shaping them to reflect who you are and what you truly want. This process isn't always easy, but it is always worth it.

Chapter 8

MANAGING REJECTION

Rejection is a deeply personal experience, and for many gay, bi, trans, and queer men, it can feel amplified by the complexities of modern dating, where intimacy and technology are tightly intertwined. In person, rejection may come in the form of a fleeting glance, a dismissive gesture, or a clear "no," but in the digital age, it takes on even more varied and sometimes confusing forms. Dating apps, social media, and messaging platforms have created new ways to reject—or be rejected—by others.

Through these platforms, new terms like *ghosting*, *orbiting*, and *breadcrumbing* have emerged. Ghosting, where someone suddenly stops all communication without explanation, is an increasingly common digital rejection strategy. It leaves the recipient confused and often without closure (Freedman et al. 2019). Breadcrumbing involves sending intermittent, flirtatious messages without any real intention of pursuing a meaningful connection (Navarro et al. 2020b). These behaviors take advantage of the anonymity and distance that technology provides, letting individuals dissolve relationships without the emotional responsibility of face-to-face communication.

Other forms of digital rejection, such as orbiting—when someone ghosts but keeps engaging with your social media content—further complicate the situation. It keeps the rejected person in an ambiguous emotional state, wondering whether the connection is truly over. These new forms of rejection can leave one feeling invisible and insignificant, reinforcing insecurities and impacting one's sense of self-worth (Barrett-Ibarria 2018).

In the context of modern dating, understanding these varied forms of rejection is crucial for emotional resilience. Whether the rejection happens face-to-face or through the screen, the feelings of inadequacy, loneliness, and helplessness can be overwhelming. However, by recognizing these behaviors for what they are—an avoidance tactic rather than a reflection of your worth—you can begin to navigate rejection in a healthier way.

AWARENESS EXERCISE

When we feel rejected, it's often more than just a fleeting emotional experience—it settles deep into our bodies. Before we explore strategies to manage rejection, let's practice some mindful reflection.

Take a deep breath, and consider the last time you felt rejected.

- Close your eyes, and scan your body. Where does the feeling of rejection land? Is it a tightness in your chest, a sinking feeling in your stomach, or perhaps tension in your jaw or shoulders? Simply notice it without judgment.

- Now, reflect on the coping behaviors you engaged in afterward. Did you turn to something soothing, like talking to a friend, journaling, or taking a walk? Or did you lean into more destructive behaviors—perhaps you numbed the pain by overindulging in food, alcohol, or doomscrolling?

- Ask yourself: *Does my coping behavior help me process the rejection, or does it distract or numb me?* Take a moment to reflect on whether these behaviors help you heal or perpetuate feelings of inadequacy. By becoming aware of how rejection shows up in our bodies and how we respond to it, we can begin to create healthier coping mechanisms.

THE EXPERIENCE

Rejection comes in many forms, and each one can have a different impact depending on the situation and context. Whether it's in person or online, the sting of rejection can trigger feelings of self-doubt, fear, and loneliness. However, the ways in which rejection is delivered can vary significantly. Understanding this spectrum of rejection can help you identify patterns and approach them with greater resilience.

ALL CONTEXTS

- **Clear communication** occurs when someone respectfully explains their disinterest by saying, "I don't think we're a good match." This direct approach provides closure, though it may still hurt.

- **A polite decline** happens when someone gently turns down an offer without being specific. An example is, "I'm not looking for anything serious right now."

- **Avoidance** occurs when someone slowly disappears from your life by frequently canceling plans or becoming emotionally distant.

- **The cold shoulder** refers to when someone ignores your attempts at communication, providing curt or disinterested replies, face-to-face or online.

- **Violent rejections** are those based explicitly and solely on race, HIV status, body size, gender expression, disability, or age.

FACE-TO-FACE

- **Vague excuses** avoid directly stating a lack of interest. For instance, "I've been really busy with work" leaves the other person unclear about the real reasons for the rejection.

- **Nonverbal cues** involve using body language or lack of engagement to signal disinterest, such as avoiding eye contact, not initiating conversation, or appearing distracted.

ONLINE

- **Ghosting** happens when someone suddenly stops all communication without explanation, disappearing from the conversation entirely (Freedman et al. 2019). This can be devastating, as it offers no closure.

- **Breadcrumbing** involves sending flirtatious, sporadic messages with no intention of moving forward. This keeps the other person emotionally invested without progressing the relationship (Navarro et al. 2020b).

- **Orbiting** occurs when someone ghosts you but keeps engaging with your social media content—liking your posts or watching your stories—without initiating any direct communication.

- **Haunting** is when someone who ghosted you reappears without explanation, perhaps liking a post or sending a random message after weeks or months of silence, creating confusion.

- **Blocking** is a final form of rejection in online spaces, where the person cuts off all contact by blocking you on social media or dating apps, making it impossible to continue the conversation or connection.

Rejection, especially in digital spaces, can be overwhelming. But it's important to remember that it's not always about you. Sometimes, people ghost or breadcrumb because they're unsure of what they want or are too uncomfortable to express their feelings honestly (Goldfarb 2017). Sometimes people ghost unintentionally because they genuinely are too busy or struggling with life circumstances, illness, or disability. Understanding these behaviors can help lessen the sting, though it doesn't eliminate the pain.

By reflecting on how rejection lands in your body and recognizing your coping strategies—whether they're helpful or harmful—you can begin to approach these experiences with more resilience and self-compassion.

DIGGING DEEPER

Sometimes, rejection taps into deeper, long-held beliefs about ourselves. Here are a few questions to help you reflect on how rejection affects you at a core level.

- Think about a time when you first felt rejected. Did that moment shape how you see yourself today? How does it compare to how you feel when you face rejection in romantic or sexual relationships now?

- Do you expect rejection before it happens? How does that affect how you act in new relationships or sexualized spaces? Do you stay guarded or avoid opening up because you assume rejection is inevitable?
- Have you noticed you're treated differently in romantic and sexual settings due to your identity (e.g., race, body size, or HIV status)? How does this impact how you approach dating and hooking up?
- Do you notice a pattern in the type of people who reject you? What do you think rejection from that "type" of person says about you and your self-worth?

MEANINGS OF REJECTION

Rejection can land in different ways depending on how it's delivered. Sometimes, it feels cruel and heartless, while other times it may hurt but was conveyed without bad intentions. Understanding the meaning you assign to rejection is key to how you process it emotionally. How do you interpret these experiences?

Rejection can be a neutral act, or it can feel personal, especially when tied to aspects of your identity like race, body size, or gender expression. Here are some common thoughts people have when they're rejected, which can shape how they process the event:

- "I'm not good enough."
- "This always happens to me."
- "I'll never find someone who wants me."
- "There's something wrong with me."
- "I'm unlovable."

While these thoughts might automatically come to mind, it's important to consider that rejection isn't always about you. Sometimes, people reject others due to their own insecurities or difficulty communicating. The rejection may not reflect your worth or desirability.

By exploring the meaning you ascribe to rejection, you can start to reshape the narrative you have around these experiences. Instead of internalizing rejection as a sign of inadequacy, you can view it as part of the dating process—something that happens, not necessarily a reflection of your value.

WHY PEOPLE GHOST

Ghosting is common in modern dating, particularly on apps and social media. It's when someone suddenly cuts off all communication without any explanation, leaving the other person wondering what went wrong. But why do people ghost? Often, it's a way to avoid confrontation or discomfort. Many people believe that by disappearing, they're sparing the other person from an awkward conversation. However, the reality is that ghosting can feel cruel and dehumanizing, as it provides no closure and leaves the recipient questioning their self-worth (LeFebvre et al. 2019). Here's an exploration of reasons people ghost:

> **Avoiding confrontation:** One of the main reasons people ghost is to avoid discomfort or an awkward conversation. They may not want to hurt your feelings directly or deal with the emotional fallout, so they choose silence to escape the situation (Freedman et al. 2019).
>
> **Uncertainty about feelings:** Sometimes people aren't sure what they want or how they feel about the relationship. Instead of working through their uncertainty or communicating their feelings, they simply disappear (Amato and Émond 2017).
>
> **Lack of emotional investment:** If someone hasn't developed a strong emotional connection, they may not feel the need to provide closure. Ghosting often happens in casual dating scenarios where one or both parties don't feel deeply invested (LeFebvre et al. 2019).
>
> **Convenience of technology:** Technology makes it easier to disappear without a trace. With a simple block or unfollow, someone can quickly remove themselves from a relationship without any immediate consequences (Navarro et al. 2020b).
>
> **Destiny beliefs:** Some people have what researchers call "destiny beliefs"—the idea that relationships are either meant to be or not. If someone believes things aren't working out, they may vanish rather than try to resolve issues, seeing the relationship as doomed from the start (Freedman et al. 2019).

People often assume they were ghosted because they did something wrong, but the reasons are usually more about the other person. While this doesn't make ghosting less painful, understanding the common reasons behind it can help you avoid internalizing it as a reflection of your own worth.

SEXUALIZING UNAVAILABILITY

In dating, especially within gay, bi, and queer communities, there can be a tendency to chase after people who seem unattainable. Sometimes, we're drawn to those who represent certain societal ideals—power, desirability, or sexual currency. This might mean seeking out men who are young, slim, tall, white, muscular, straight-passing, wealthy, or popular. The attraction to these traits can be wrapped up in our own longing for power or validation.

Take Santiago, a twenty-eight-year-old Venezuelan American. He's short, racialized, and generally considered attractive. Yet, Santiago often seeks out white, bodybuilder-type men and experiences frequent rejection. When his therapist asks what it would mean to him if these men reciprocated interest, Santiago says, "It would mean I'm attractive; I've made it." His therapist reflects back, "So, proximity to whiteness and muscularity would feel like a sign of progress and security to you?"

As Santiago continues, he realizes that these rejections lead him to internalize feelings of unworthiness. He starts to see how his desire for certain types of men—those who embody societal ideals—is reinforcing his own insecurities about race and attractiveness. The repeated rejection from this "type" of man has impacted him, leading to feelings of inadequacy and self-doubt.

It's worth reflecting on the types of men and masculinities you're drawn to. Are you often chasing those who seem unattainable? How often do you face rejection from that particular "type"? What impact does this have on your self-esteem and emotional well-being? While there's nothing wrong with being attracted to someone different from yourself, it's important to consider whether that attraction is tied to a deeper longing for validation or power.

THOUGHT ANALYSIS: GHOSTED

1. **Situation:** You've been ghosted after a few promising dates. Everything seemed to be going well, but suddenly, they stopped responding and disappeared.

2. **Feelings and behaviors:** You feel hurt, abandoned, and confused. You might start blaming yourself or replaying every conversation, wondering if you did something wrong. You might feel unworthy, anxious, or rejected. You may begin overanalyzing the situation, or even start reaching out to them repeatedly, hoping for a response.

3. **Prominent unhelpful thought:** "They ghosted me because I'm not good enough. This always happens to me. I'll never find someone who really likes me."

4. **Evaluate:** I don't actually know why they ghosted me, and there's a chance it is about them. If this is happening to me repeatedly, it might also be about the culture of dating.

5. **Balanced alternative thought:** "Being ghosted hurts, but it doesn't mean I'm unworthy of love or connection. This says more about their communication skills than about me."

RIGHTEOUS REFRAMING

Rejection, especially when it involves racism, fatphobia, HIV stigma, femmephobia, or ableism, can feel deeply personal and painful. It's important to affirm that these experiences are unacceptable and can leave lasting emotional wounds. However, by reframing how we perceive these rejections, we can challenge the narratives we've internalized and rebuild a sense of self-worth.

Let's take a look at some examples of rejection and how to reframe them with balanced, alternative thoughts:

- **Ableism**

    Initial thought: "They rejected me because of my disability. No one will ever want to be with me because I'm different."

    Reframed thought: "Their rejection reflects their inability to appreciate my value, not my worth. My disability is part of me, and I deserve to be loved for who I am."

- **HIV Stigma**

    Initial thought: "They stopped talking to me after I disclosed my HIV status. I'll always be seen as damaged or unsafe."

    Reframed thought: "Their reaction is based on ignorance, not my health status. I am worthy of love and connection, and I deserve someone who respects and understands my journey."

- **Fatphobia**

    Initial thought: "I was rejected because of my size. I'll never be attractive enough."

    Reframed thought: "Their rejection says more about their narrow view of beauty than about my worth. I deserve someone who appreciates my body and sees me as a whole person."

- **Femmephobia**

    Initial thought: "They don't like me because I'm too femme. I'll never be masculine enough to be desired."

    Reframed thought: "Femme is beautiful and powerful. If someone can't see that, they're not the right person for me. I deserve to be loved for my authentic self."

- **Racism**

    Initial thought: "They rejected me because of my race. I'll never be good enough in a society that values whiteness over everything."

    Reframed thought: "Their bias is not a reflection of my worth. I deserve to be with someone who embraces and celebrates my identity."

These reframed thoughts don't diminish the reality of how hurtful rejection can be. They also shift the narrative from self-blame to self-affirmation.

Digging Deeper

- When you're rejected, does it reinforce a belief that you're not good enough? How has rejection shaped your view of yourself? What core belief about your worth do you hold, and how have they influenced your dating experiences?

- Think about a time when you rejected someone. How did you feel afterward? Did you feel shame, guilt, or maybe even power or relief? Consider why you felt that way. Did you feel empathy for the person you rejected? Did it remind you of a time you were rejected?

- When you've rejected someone, were you trying to avoid discomfort or confrontation? Or perhaps leaning into your own exclusionary biases? Understanding your motivations for rejecting others can offer insight into how you handle rejection yourself.

EMPTY CHAIR: WOUNDED EGO

The ego—our sense of self—often carries the pain, confusion, and self-doubt that arise when we feel unwanted or dismissed. This exercise will help you explore how rejection impacts your sense of self-worth, offering space to process those emotions.

Step 1: Create the Space

- Take a moment to sit comfortably.
- Imagine that in the empty chair in front of you sits the version of yourself that feels rejected, hurt, and wounded. This is the part of you that internalizes rejection and takes it as a personal reflection of your worth.

Step 2: Speak to Your Wounded Ego

- Begin by addressing the person in the empty chair.
- You might say, "Hello, Wounded Ego. You represent the part of me that feels rejected and unwanted because of... [mention a recent experience of rejection]."
- As you speak, notice any sensations in your body—tightness, heaviness, or tension. These feelings are valid and real.
- Continue speaking. What do you want to say about how rejection has impacted you?

- Acknowledge how it has affected your self-esteem and sense of worth. Are there specific thoughts or memories that come up when you think about being rejected? What beliefs about yourself are reinforced by this experience?

Step 3: Switch Chairs and Embody Your Wounded Ego

- Switch places and sit in the empty chair. You are now embodying the Wounded Ego.
- Speak from this place of hurt.
- You might say, "I feel small, unworthy, or inadequate because of what happened. I believe I'm not good enough because I was rejected." Allow yourself to express the raw emotions tied to this wounded part of you.

Step 4: Conclusion

- Switch back to your original seat. Take a deep breath.
- Acknowledge that this part of you has been trying to protect you from further pain by carrying the weight of rejection.
- Thank the Wounded Ego for trying to shield you from hurt, and gently remind it that rejection is not always about your worth.
- Finally, make an agreement with the Wounded Ego.
- You might say, "I understand that you feel hurt, but I also know that rejection doesn't define my value. I will work on not letting these experiences undermine my self-worth, and I will honor the parts of me that feel wounded without letting them control how I see myself."

This exercise invites you to engage with the embodied pain of rejection while creating space for healing and self-compassion. As you move forward, reflect on how you can be kinder to yourself during moments of rejection and separate your worth from the judgments of others.

Chapter 9

BODY-CONSCIOUS CULTURE

If you're seeking connection with other GBTQ guys, you're likely doing it online or in spaces that cater to queer men. The subculture of GBTQ guys has norms and messages not only about connection-seeking, but also about which bodies are seen as attractive and desirable.

WHAT IS BODY IMAGE?

Body image is fundamentally how you see and feel about your body, particularly its appearance and what you perceive as attractive. This concept splits into two distinct parts: objective realities and mental images. Objective realities are the tangible, measurable aspects of your body—height, weight, and body shape. These are factual and not open to interpretation. In contrast, your mental image of your body is more subjective, influenced by personal experiences, emotional states, and societal standards.

Your body image does not exist in isolation. It is heavily influenced by external forces. Pornography, dance parties, targeted ads, social media, and others' self-criticisms about bodies all shape how you view your own. These influences often present an idealized, unachievable standard of beauty that can deeply impact how you see yourself.

AWARENESS EXERCISE

What part of your body are you usually most aware of when you try on clothes or get dressed in the morning? What parts of your body are you most critical of when you are in queer spaces? Really feel these questions in your body as you let the answers emerge.

DIGGING DEEPER

This part is about you and your own journey with your body. Take a moment to think about these questions:

1. How did you feel about your body when you were growing up? Did you ever stand in front of the mirror, comparing yourself to others, wondering why you looked the way you did?

2. How did your relationship with your body change after you became engaged in GBTQ communities? Did you start to see your body as a project, something to work on and improve?

3. How do you balance the pride you feel about your identity with feelings about your body? It's complicated, right? Sometimes, the more you try to celebrate your queerness, the harder you are on how you look!

These questions aren't easy, and they might bring up a lot of emotions. That's okay. This is your time to think about how you got to where you are with your body. It's all about understanding your feelings, so you can start feeling better about who you are, inside and out.

CULTURAL IMPRINTS

Though GBTQ communities offer vital safe havens from the harshness of a homophobic world, sometimes these communities hold up a mirror where a certain physique seems to be the price of admission. Engage deeply with the following list of factors that may contribute to your own relationship to your body and GBTQ men's body-conscious culture.

1. **The impact of the AIDS epidemic**

   During the height of the AIDS crisis, the visibility of HIV-positive gay men and the physical manifestations of illness became conflated with the broader image of the gay man. This period left a lasting imprint, prompting many within the community to embrace fitness not only as a health goal, but also as a statement against stigma.

   Pause and reflect: How does historical context shape your perceptions of health and strength, particularly in the GBTQ community?

What personal or collective memories might you be countering through your physical appearance?

2. **Milestone rebellion**

    You've already considered what heteronormative milestones are and how they might exclude you. If you're invested in having a particular body type, perhaps that is a way to make yourself more visible in heterosexual and family settings. Perhaps it's an unconscious rebellion against imposed milestones, and makes you feel superior to or on an equal plane with your heterosexual counterparts.

    Pause and reflect: Has an emphasis on your physique been a visible signifier of your different life trajectory from your straight peers or family of origin?

3. **Responses to bullying and scrutiny**

    Children are bullied for many reasons. If you were, it may have been related to your gender expression—the way you dressed, walked, or talked—or your proximity to femininity—your favorite subjects, interests, and groups of friends. Bullying can be a profoundly painful experience that GBTQ guys might spend a lifetime trying to prevent or compensate for. Muscular and toned bodies often signify strength and sometimes define what's attractive. If your masculinity has been attacked in the past, a focus on how your body looks now might be a source of social and sexual currency.

    Pause and reflect: How have past experiences of bullying or scrutiny shaped your relationship with your body? What defenses have you built around your self-image to combat societal or internal negativity?

4. **Unconscious rivalries**

    Competition is central to capitalist culture—the same culture that sells us ideas about what it means to be healthy or unhealthy. Because every detail of your emotional life isn't conscious, there's a good chance your efforts to go to the gym or eat well in order to "be healthy" are also driven by unconscious rivalries with other gay men or gym goers. If you've ever felt that declining a dessert was a kind of victory, you've likely endorsed a kind of competition with others.

Pause and reflect: How much of your pursuit of muscularity or thinness is driven by personal health goals, and how much is driven by competition with others?

5. **Curating masculinity to facilitate feminine expression**

   Expressing femininity does not feel safe for many men, and GBTQ guys are not an exception. As a result, you may find that accentuating traditional masculine traits through bodybuilding lets you express femininity in other realms, such as performance art or drag. An example of this can be seen in places like Puerto Vallarta, where it's easy to spot the chiseled "gay clones" whose gym memberships allow them to confidently wear thongs and long, flowy cloaks on the beach.

   Pause and reflect: How does conforming to masculine ideals give you "permission" to express your femininity? Can your masculinity coexist with genuine feminine expression? What challenges arise in this balance?

6. **Fatphobia: identifying with the aggressor**

   "Identifying with the aggressor" is a psychological concept where an individual adopts the values or behaviors of those they perceive as threats, as a way to cope with fear or insecurity. This behavior can manifest as embracing societal standards that favor muscularity or thinness, even if it conflicts with personal health or self-acceptance. If you are fairly satisfied with yourself but think you'd be a better person if you went to the gym more or restricted your diet, this may be you.

   Pause and reflect: Have you absorbed societal standards to an unhelpful degree? Might you have identified with the very forces that feel oppressive when it comes to your body image?

7. **Compromise formation**

   In psychoanalysis, "compromise formation" refers to the process of developing behaviors that reconcile internal desires with societal demands. This is a sophisticated defense mechanism. In this context, GBTQ guys may pursue physical fitness to fulfill the need for personal recognition in a predominantly straight world, while also adhering to societal standards of attractiveness and success.

Pause and reflect: How do you balance your authenticity with societal expectations around masculinity and body image? Is there a chance experiences with homophobia influenced your approach to fitness and physical appearance?

8. **Sexual currency and peer influence**

   You've likely been on the apps and social media. You know very well what body types get celebrated. In the realm of sex, dating, and social interactions, your thumbnail photo is used to quickly "assess" your physical appearance and ascribe social worth and desirability to your persona. It's valuable to resist these harsh and negative evaluations by people you don't know, but it's also useful to acknowledge the ways you might invest in your appearance for their approval.

   Pause and reflect: Do you evaluate some body shapes and sizes as more desirable than others? How might this evaluation harm yourself or other GBTQ guys? Consider your internal reaction when friends discuss their bodies and regimens. How does that shape your own body image and the pressures you feel?

ENVY AND SHAME

In the world you're living in, it's tough not to look around and see things you wish you had. It's normal to see other guys—maybe at the gym or on social media—and feel a tug of envy. Maybe they have the kind of muscles you've been working toward, or they just seem to be "put together."

Envy is like a mirror that shows you what you think you're missing. It can make you feel small, even if you're doing great things in your own life. And it's tricky because it often travels with its shadowy friend: shame. Envy makes you want what others have, and shame makes you feel inferior for not having it. This is a painful place to be.

IF / THEN STATEMENTS

If/then statements in cognitive behavior therapy are like the mental pathways we create to predict how we feel about ourselves and the world around us. They often go something like this: "If I don't have this kind of body, then I won't be happy or loved." But what if you could rewrite these statements? What if you could change the rules?

Let's unravel some common if/then statements around body image. These might sound familiar:

"If I don't have a firm, round butt, then I won't be attractive to potential partners." It's a statement that can make you feel inadequate every time you try on clothes or compare yourself to images in the media.

> **Instead, consider:** "If my body lets me interact with the world and the people I care about, then I can be grateful for it and the journey it's been through."

"If my shoulders aren't broad and strong, then I'm not masculine enough." This kind of thinking can make you push too hard at the gym or feel lesser than when you're out with friends.

> **Instead, consider:** "If my shoulders can carry the burdens of my daily life—physically or metaphorically—then they are powerful in their own unique way."

"If my arms aren't bulging with muscles, then I look weak." It's a thought that might discourage you from wearing certain shirts or participating in activities.

> **Instead, consider:** "If my arms allow me to hug the people I love or do my favorite activities, then they are perfect as they are."

"If my penis isn't big, or I don't have one, then I'm not man enough or capable of satisfying a partner." This is a worry that can cause anxiety and self-doubt, but it's not the truth.

> **Instead, consider:** "If I can communicate with my partner and connect on multiple levels, then intimacy will be fulfilling, regardless of size or parts."

"If I don't have chiseled pecs and a flat stomach, then I'm not fit to be seen shirtless." This can suck the joy out of summer or a trip to the beach.

> **Instead, consider:** "If I can breathe and my heart beats, then my chest and stomach are doing exactly what they need to do."

These new if/then statements aren't about denying your desires for your body; they're about changing the belief that your worth is tied solely to appearance. They're about transforming your perspective to one of acceptance and celebration of what your body can do and the person you are.

EMPTY CHAIR: BODY PARTS

Here's a slightly more challenging task: take a step away from thinking about your body to actually be in it. The following Empty Chair exercise is a dialogue with a body part you often criticize. The goal is increased empathy and self-compassion.

Many of these steps come with example dialogues, but feel free to say whatever comes to you in the moment.

Step 1: Create the Space

- Arrange two chairs facing each other in a quiet, private space.
- Sit in one chair, and imagine that the body part you often criticize (e.g., your arms) is personified and sitting in the other chair.

Step 2: Speak to the Body Part

- Begin by expressing how you typically feel about this body part.

    "I always feel embarrassed about how you [my arms] look in T-shirts. I wish you were more toned."

- Tell the body part how you imagine your life would be different if it were more desirable.

- "If you just worked harder or stood out more, I'd have more confidence."

- Share a story about when you first became hyperaware of the body part and when it let you down.

- "I remember being in twelfth grade gym class, lifting weights. A classmate said he was surprised by how much 'the tiny twigs' [referring to you] could lift. It may have been a compliment, but it made me feel bad. I began to notice other people's arms and how they fit nicely into those 'muscle fit' shirts. That's when I really felt like you let me down."

Step 3: Switch Chairs and Embody the Body Part

- Switch chairs and speak *as the body part* to the empty chair that now represents you [the person].
- Describe how you experience the criticism and pressure to look a different way.

   "When you focus so much on how I look, it feels like you're missing the hard work I do. It hurts when the only attention I get is for not being enough or not fitting into societal ideals."

- Tell your larger being what you try to do for him on a daily basis.

   "Every day, I support you in everything you do. From lifting groceries to hugging loved ones, I'm always working to help you live your life fully, even if I don't look exactly how you wish. Still, I feel awful that you're disappointed in me."

- Ask your larger being for some self-compassion and specific forms of care

   "Maybe we can start appreciating our strength together, not just in the gym but in taking care of each other. Let's focus on nourishing ourselves with healthy foods and enough rest, instead of always pushing so hard. I'd love for you to grieve what I'm not so we can start appreciating how we do help each other."

Step 4: Conclusion

- Return to your original seat and take a deep breath to ground yourself.
- Thank your body part for the conversation.

FINAL REFLECTIONS

- During your conversation, what did you learn about your body's role in your life?

- How might you reframe critical thoughts into affirmations that celebrate your body's function and uniqueness?

- What can this exercise teach you about acceptance and the journey toward body positivity?

Chapter 10

ENDINGS IN QUEER LOVE

Breakups can be emotionally devastating, especially for GBTQ guys, who can sometimes feel like their world offers more opportunities for casual encounters than longer-term relationships. Research indicates that relationship endings can have significant mental health impacts, including depression, anxiety, and feelings of loss (Gilbert and Sifers 2011). These emotional responses often mirror the deep emotional attachment we form in relationships, which when broken, can leave us feeling as though we've lost a part of ourselves. In GBTQ relationships, breakups may also be intertwined with struggles around identity, self-worth, and societal acceptance, intensifying the pain.

It's important to acknowledge that breakups are not just about the loss of a romantic partner; they can also mean the loss of a community, particularly in smaller queer circles. Breakups can evoke identity threats, especially for those whose relationships were significant in their coming-out journey (Jaspal 2015). Breakups may also trigger insecurities about future relationships, particularly given stigma against queer love, making the grief process even more complicated.

However, despite the pain, breakups are a normal developmental challenge. Learning to navigate and cope with the emotional fallout can lead to significant personal growth. Understanding that these feelings of despair—while difficult—are temporary and part of the healing process can be a key factor in recovery.

QUEER VS. STRAIGHT RELATIONSHIPS

GBTQ relationships are fundamentally different from their straight counterparts in several key ways. For many GBTQ individuals, relationships are not only about romantic connection, but also play a significant role in self-discovery, identity, and community building. These relationships often provide a space for individuals to express parts of themselves that may have been hidden or suppressed due to societal pressures or expectations (Jaspal 2015). A relationship might even coincide with the coming-out process, making it part of a larger journey toward personal authenticity.

Unlike straight relationships, which tend to follow the "relationship escalator"—an expected progression from dating to cohabitation, marriage, and children—GBTQ relationships often resist this script. The queer community has long challenged traditional relationship norms, embracing nontraditional structures such as open relationships, polyamory, or co-parenting without marriage (Cloud 2008). These relationships tend to be more fluid and adaptable, reflecting the diverse and evolving needs of the individuals involved.

Further, the GBTQ community often places a strong emphasis on the idea of chosen family. As many face rejection from biological family members due to their queerness, their romantic and platonic relationships may carry extra emotional weight. This sense of chosen family can make a breakup feel even more significant, as it may also disrupt one's larger support network (Blair 2021).

When GBTQ relationships end, it's often not just the loss of a romantic partner, but a loss of a critical space for self-expression and community connection.

AWARENESS EXERCISE

Reflect on where your ideas about relationships and breakups come from. What stories were you told about how relationships are supposed to work? Were you influenced by what you saw in your family, your friends, or TV shows and movies?

Now, think about how those stories have shaped your expectations of how breakups "should" happen. Do you believe one person is supposed to be the "bad guy" in the breakup? Is there an assumption that it's always the other person's fault or that relationships are failures if they don't last forever?

How do these expectations show up in your own breakups? Did you take on a specific role—like the "heartbreaker" or the "heartbroken"? How did those roles affect the way you processed the end of the relationship?

HOLLYWOOD BREAKUPS

Popular culture, particularly movies and TV shows, often portrays breakups in predictable, dramatized ways. In romantic comedies, breakups are usually caused by misunderstandings, mismatched life goals, infidelity, or a lack of communication. These depictions imply that breakups are obstacles to be overcome on the way to "true love"—often framed as heteronormative, monogamous, and long lasting.

Hollywood teaches us that breakups are inherently negative. They're often shown as devastating, with an inevitable silver lining where the main character grows as a person or finds someone "better." These stories follow a familiar narrative arc: heartbreak, self-doubt, a period of reflection, and then personal transformation or romantic success with "The One." The protagonist is expected to endure heartbreak as a necessary step toward ultimate romantic fulfillment, reinforcing the idea that a successful life requires a long-term partner. Additionally, Hollywood breakups typically cast one person as the villain and the other as the victim, encouraging a narrative of blame. This binary thinking can make it harder to process breakups in real life, where both people may simply grow apart or want different things.

GBTQ BREAKUPS

Breakups in GBTQ relationships can be especially tough because you're navigating a unique set of challenges. On top of the usual heartbreak, you might also be dealing with societal stigma or internalized homophobia, which can make it even more painful. It's easy to feel like the end of a relationship confirms some of your negative beliefs about love or belonging (Jaspal 2015).

In smaller queer communities, breakups can feel even more complicated. You might still see your ex at social events, in queer spaces, or even within your own friend group, making it harder to get the space you need to heal (Blair 2021). For some, especially bisexual men, a breakup might stir up questions about where you "fit" in terms of dating—whether you're navigating both queer and straight spaces, or figuring out what comes next for you (Oakley 2020).

Despite all of this, there's hope. One of the strengths of the GBTQ community is its focus on chosen family and maintaining connections, even after a breakup. It's possible to stay friends with an ex or reshape the relationship in a way that still honors the bond you've shared. You can move forward, even if your romantic relationship has ended.

PURPOSE OF RELATIONSHIPS

The idea that relationships are only successful if they follow a straight path to marriage and children is deeply ingrained in our culture. But in queer relationships, success often looks different. It's about connection, growth, and being present with someone for as long as it serves both of you. Sometimes, a relationship can be incredibly meaningful even if it doesn't last forever.

Let's consider the story of Jose and Pieter, a queer couple in Winnipeg. They've been together for eight years, living a loving and committed life with their two dogs. Over time, their romantic connection has faded, and they're now seeking different things in life. Even though they've decided to part ways, they don't see their relationship as a failure. Instead, they cherish the love they've shared and want to continue supporting one another, embracing the idea of conscious uncoupling.

For Jose and Pieter, their relationship was successful because it gave them love, growth, and companionship when they needed it most. Now, they're choosing to honor what they've built while moving in different directions. Splitting up is not a failure but a natural evolution of their connection.

The purpose of your relationships—like Jose and Pieter's—might not fit into traditional molds, but they're still equally valid. Queer relationships are often about creating your own definitions of love, and sometimes that means recognizing when it's time to let go while still honoring what you've shared.

DIGGING DEEPER

Breakups often bring up deep, sometimes unresolved emotions that go beyond the immediate relationship. Let's reflect on how your past experiences with endings, departures, or transitions might be influencing how you handle breakups today.

1. When you think about the end of this relationship, does it bring up feelings related to other departures in your life? Maybe a friendship that faded or a time when you had to leave a community? How do these experiences compare?

2. Has this ending changed how you view yourself or your worth? Do you feel like it reinforces any long-standing insecurities?

3. What role did you play in this breakup? Think about how you showed up in the relationship and how the breakup happened.

This kind of reflection allows you to process not just the immediate hurt, but also the underlying feelings tied to other experiences in your life.

THOUGHT ANALYSIS: THE BREAKUP

Let's break down your thoughts and feelings about a breakup you've experienced using a thought analysis. Use the example below as a template.

1. **Situation:** My partner of one year ended the relationship to focus on himself because he felt he lost his sense of self.

2. **Feelings and behaviors:** You might feel rejected, hurt, or even blame yourself. Perhaps you're replaying the breakup in your mind or isolating yourself from friends.

3. **Prominent unhelpful thought:** "It's my fault he lost himself. I wasn't enough, and I'll never make a relationship work."

4. **Evaluate:** Is it really true that you caused him to lose himself? Could this be more about his personal journey? Relationships involve two people, and it's not fair to put all the blame on yourself.

5. **Balanced alternative thought:** "This breakup is painful, but it doesn't define my worth. My partner needed space to focus on himself, and that's valid. I can grow from this and find a healthy relationship in the future."

CONSCIOUS UNCOUPLING

In the context of GBTQ relationships, the concept of conscious uncoupling offers an approach to breakups that emphasizes respect, healing, and a focus on personal growth, rather than viewing the relationship's end as a failure

(Salehuddin et al. 2024). The idea is to honor the relationship for what it was and transform the dissolution into an opportunity for self-discovery and mutual understanding.

Here's how to approach conscious uncoupling after a breakup (adapted from Salehuddin et al. 2024):

1. **Find emotional freedom:** When a relationship ends, particularly for queer individuals, emotions tied to identity, rejection, and societal pressures may feel overwhelming. First, allow yourself space to feel these emotions and channel them toward self-empowerment, instead of letting them spiral into self-blame or societal shame. Embrace your authentic self by reflecting on how this breakup has clarified your values, desires, and personal needs.

2. **Reclaim your power and your life:** Take ownership of the breakup narrative. Rather than viewing it as a "failure," shift the focus toward what you've learned about yourself, your boundaries, and your relationship patterns. Consider how the relationship might have served as a safe space to explore identity, while now paving the way to new self-growth.

3. **Break the pattern, heal your heart:** Look closely at any repeated relationship dynamics or harmful beliefs that may have contributed to the end of the relationship. For GBTQ individuals, this could involve internalized homophobia, fears of abandonment, or societal pressures surrounding queer relationships, which may sabotage future connections.

4. **Become a love alchemist:** Take responsibility for transforming lingering hurt or anger into compassion—for yourself and your former partner. Acknowledge the strengths and beautiful moments of the relationship while accepting that both of you are on separate, evolving journeys.

5. **Create your happily-even-after life:** Last, consciously uncoupling doesn't mean severing ties completely. GBTQ communities are often small and interconnected, which means it's possible (and often necessary) to maintain connections, whether as friends or simply as part of the same social circles. Set boundaries that honor both your healing

and your former partner's, finding ways to move forward without animosity.

In short, conscious uncoupling allows GBTQ people to view relationship endings as transitions, rather than failures. By embracing this philosophy, you can honor what the relationship taught you while nurturing personal growth and fostering healthier dynamics in the future.

EMPTY CHAIR: FAREWELL

In this exercise, we'll use the Empty Chair technique to help you process post-relationship grief. You might be feeling anger, self-blame, or frustration that the pain of the breakup isn't going away quickly. This exercise lets you dialogue with your grief and give it space to be heard.

Step 1: Create the Space

- Take a seat in front of an empty chair.

- Imagine your grief sitting in the chair across from you—representing all the emotions you've been carrying since the breakup. Your grief is tied to the relationship you lost, the hopes you had, and the love that was shared.

Step 2: Speak to Your Grief

- Start by addressing your grief directly:

    "Grief, I feel angry that you won't go away. I'm frustrated that I'm still hurting even after the relationship has ended. I blame myself sometimes for things that went wrong, and I feel stuck. Why won't you let me move on?"

Step 3: Switch Chairs and Embody Your Grief

- Switch seats. Speak as your grief, expressing what it wants you to know:

    "I'm here because I'm holding onto the parts of your relationship that mattered. I'm carrying the lessons, love, and memories that are still important. I'm not here to make you suffer, but to remind you that what you experienced was real and valuable. This relationship wasn't wasted—it contributed to who you are now. Let me help you frame this ending as a success. Nothing done in queer love is wasted."

Step 4: Conclusion

- Return to your original seat. Reflect on what your grief has said to you. Can you see how it's holding the valuable parts of your relationship?

- Thank your grief for reminding you that while the relationship has ended, it wasn't a failure. Allow yourself to feel that it mattered, and that it's okay to carry those lessons with you.

- Take a deep breath, and when you're ready, say your final words to your grief:

"Thank you for helping me hold onto the parts of this relationship that were important. I know I don't need to stay stuck in the pain, and I'll honor what this relationship brought into my life."

Chapter 11

BOUNDARY VIOLATIONS

Think of personal boundaries as the walls of a house. The walls protect your personal space and belongings, letting in people you trust while keeping out those who may harm you. A boundary violation is like someone breaking a window or barging in uninvited. Even if they don't take anything, the intrusion leaves you feeling vulnerable and unsafe, questioning your trust and sense of security. Over time, repeated boundary violations can weaken your emotional "house," making it harder to feel comfortable and safe in your relationships. Like a home, if boundaries are constantly crossed, you may feel overwhelmed, disrespected, and in need of repair.

Personal boundaries are the limits and rules individuals set for themselves within relationships. They help define where you end and others begin, providing a sense of control and comfort. Having healthy boundaries means knowing when to say "no" and how to have close relationships without compromising your sense of self. Boundaries also influence how satisfied you are with how your resources—such as time, energy, and emotions—are used. They are critical for ensuring that relationships and activities are sustainable over the long term, as they protect your emotional, mental, and physical well-being.

AWARENESS EXERCISE

Close your eyes and imagine yourself as a small but sturdy house with four walls. For each decade of your life, consider what the state of the house is and what kinds of boundary violations it's had to endure. You might find that some walls are strong and secure, while others have cracks or breaks. Take time to walk through each decade and reflect on your experiences.

Here are a few examples:

- **Age 10:** Fairly safe, but one wall is cracked from comments about my masculinity.
- **Age 20:** One wall is shattered by bullying in college.
- **Age 30:** My walls are reinforced, but keeping my HIV status private has been hard.
- **Age 40:** Respectful friends make me feel like the house is in good shape.
- **Age 50:** A breakup comes with some bad behavior from my ex-partner, leaving one wall a bit shaky.
- **Age 60:** Exploited by someone on a dating app; experienced drug-facilitated assault, making me feel like parts of the house are crumbling.
- **Age 70:** Siblings plan a holiday dinner and don't invite my partner, leaving one wall completely exposed.
- **Age 80:** Experiences of ageism diminish my wisdom, making me feel like the house is smaller and less appreciated.

MASCULINITIES AND VULNERABILITIES

When discussing boundary violations among GBTQ guys, it's essential to recognize the unique ways that societal norms around masculinity are involved. GBTQ men often face extra challenges due to societal expectations that discourage vulnerability, emotional expression, and open conversations about consent and harm. Healing from boundary violations requires nuanced and specific conversations that acknowledge these unique experiences.

RAPE CULTURE

Within the broader culture of toxic masculinity, men are often socialized to view sexual encounters as "wins" or conquests. This narrative is particularly strong in GBTQ communities, with hypersexualized ideals often heightened by hookup apps and sexualized spaces (García-Gómez 2024). Therefore, many men may downplay or ignore boundary violations, even when they feel violated, because acknowledging the harm conflicts with societal messages that men should not be victims.

In environments that prioritize sexual success, GBTQ men may also feel internalized pressure to deny their own victimization, which can result in underreporting sexual violence (Hindes and Fileborn 2020). This cultural conditioning leaves many men without the language or support to navigate their experiences of harm, further isolating them from conversations about healing.

COMPLICATED NARRATIVES OF INTERGENERATIONAL ENCOUNTERS

Some men experience relationships that others may label as inappropriate as empowering or healing, especially intergenerationally, when young GBTQ men enter sexual relationships with older partners. In some cases, these encounters are seen as rites of passage or moments of sexual exploration, but they can also carry elements of coercion or manipulation (Hequembourg et al. 2014). The complexity of these narratives can make it difficult to categorize these relationships in black-and-white, but it's important to create space for all individuals to reflect on whether their boundaries were respected and how the experience affected them.

In some cases, men may struggle to define their experiences as boundary violations because the encounter doesn't fit traditional ideas of abuse. This highlights the importance of discussing these gray areas in GBTQ spaces, where the lines between consent, coercion, and empowerment can blur.

CONSENT IN GBTQ COMMUNITIES

While there has been a growing emphasis on affirmative consent in heterosexual communities, discussions about consent in GBTQ spaces remain limited. Hookup apps and sexualized spaces often prioritize nonverbal cues or brief profile descriptions, leaving little room for open and clear communication about boundaries (García-Gómez 2024). This creates an environment where consent can be misunderstood or disregarded entirely.

For many GBTQ men, the idea of direct verbal consent may feel foreign or uncomfortable, because these conversations often conflict with the unspoken sexual scripts they've internalized (Sternin et al. 2021). We need more robust conversations about what consent looks like in queer contexts, where power dynamics, social pressures, and injuries to masculinity can complicate communication.

GAY CULTURAL NORMS

Anonymous sex, a common feature of many GBTQ subcultures, offers both freedom and risk. While it provides a space for sexual exploration away from heteronormative expectations, it can also make it more difficult to assert boundaries and protect oneself from harm—especially in environments where casual sex is the norm or expectations around consent are not explicit (Salter et al. 2020).

The normalization of anonymous sex in gay bars, saunas, and online platforms creates a complex dynamic where asserting one's boundaries can feel out of place. This leaves men vulnerable to nonconsensual encounters, which are often dismissed as just "part of the culture" (Gibbs and Baldwin-White 2022). Addressing the nuanced vulnerabilities that GBTQ men face in these spaces requires a shift in how we think about sexual agency and the importance of explicit, ongoing consent in every encounter.

By integrating these complex conversations into GBTQ communities, we can help men move beyond the cultural scripts that limit their ability to talk openly about boundary violations and instead foster environments where healing and vulnerability are embraced.

TYPES OF VIOLATIONS

Let's take stock of the boundary violations you may have endured, or even perpetrated. The goal is to reflect on how these experiences have shaped your core beliefs about yourself, others, and the world. As you move through the different types of violations, ask yourself: What have I endured? How have these experiences shaped my beliefs about myself and my relationships?

Afterward, you'll consider what restructuring these core beliefs might look like. Restructuring refers to identifying unhelpful or negative beliefs and working toward more compassionate, realistic ones.

Take your time moving through each type of violation. Remember, healing begins with awareness.

PHYSICAL VIOLATIONS

These can include unwanted touch, invading personal space, and inappropriate physical contact. These boundary violations often feel like direct attacks on your physical autonomy and comfort, leading to feelings of vulnerability and powerlessness.

- A young, gay high school student experiences unwanted touching from a classmate during gym, who uses it as a joke to publicly humiliate him.

- A bisexual man at a family gathering is hugged tightly by an older relative after repeatedly expressing discomfort with close physical contact.

- A trans man in his twenties feels uncomfortable when someone in a bar keeps leaning in too close while speaking, despite him stepping back multiple times.

Pause and reflect: Think about any physical violations you've encountered. How did they make you feel about your body and your right to physical space? Have these experiences led you to feel unsafe or disrespected in certain environments? How might you reclaim your sense of physical autonomy by setting clear boundaries and practicing assertiveness in uncomfortable situations?

EMOTIONAL VIOLATIONS

These can include sharing personal information without consent, disregarding your feelings, or using guilt-tripping tactics. These violations often strike at your emotional core, leaving you feeling exposed, misunderstood, or manipulated.

- A nonbinary teen confides in a family member about their gender identity, only for that person to share it with others without permission.

- A bisexual man in his fifties is at a community event when someone brings up private details about his past relationship struggles, leading to embarrassment.

- A trans man is guilt-tripped by a partner into staying in a toxic relationship by being told that no one else would truly understand him.

Pause and reflect: Have you ever experienced emotional violations? How have they impacted your trust in others or your ability to share personal information? How might you protect your emotional boundaries going forward? What might healthy communication look like for you?

PROFESSIONAL VIOLATIONS

These can include dual relationships, overstepping roles, or sharing confidential information. These types of violations can blur the lines between personal and professional life, making it difficult to navigate relationships with colleagues or professionals.

- A young gay man receives therapy from a friend from a shared social group, blurring the boundaries of professional and personal support.

- A bisexual man in his workplace is asked by his boss to talk about his personal life in front of coworkers, overstepping professional boundaries by making his sexual orientation a subject of discussion.

- A trans man in a support group learns that the group leader shared details of his transition journey with another person without consent.

Pause and reflect: Consider any professional violations you've experienced. How did they affect your work environment or your sense of professionalism? How might you establish clearer boundaries at work or with professionals to ensure privacy and respect?

DIGITAL BOUNDARY VIOLATIONS

These can include cyberstalking, sharing personal information online, or sending unsolicited content. In our increasingly connected world, digital violations can feel pervasive and difficult to escape, often leading to feelings of helplessness and an invasion of privacy.

- A gay man discovers an ex-partner is obsessively watching his online activity and comments on everything, all the time.

- A trans man in his thirties faces harassment from a stranger who follows him across social media, sending invasive messages about his transition.

- A bisexual man's ex posts about their past relationship, including intimate details, without his consent, leading to public embarrassment.

Pause and reflect: Have you faced digital boundary violations? How did these experiences affect your sense of safety online? Reflect on the importance of setting digital boundaries, such as controlling who can access your personal information or limiting interactions with individuals who do not respect your boundaries.

SEXUAL BOUNDARY VIOLATIONS

These can include sexual assault, intimate partner violence, childhood abuse, drug-facilitated abuse, or inappropriate norms in sexualized spaces. These violations often leave deep scars, affecting how you view your body, sexuality, and relationships.

- A gay man in his twenties is sexually assaulted by a partner, who ignores his repeated refusals during an intimate encounter.

- A bisexual man in his fifties is assaulted at a social event, where someone uses his sexual orientation as justification for nonconsensual touching.

- A bisexual teenager is sexually abused by a family member, making it difficult for him to embrace his queerness and making him question the authenticity of his relationships.

- A gay man in his thirties carries the trauma of sexual abuse by a trusted family friend when he was a child, impacting his ability to trust in adult relationships.

- A gay soldier experiences sexual assault from a fellow servicemember, feeling powerless and isolated due to military hierarchy.

- A trans man visiting a doctor experiences inappropriate comments and touching during an examination that crosses professional lines.

- A gay man is drugged at a party and later wakes up realizing he was sexually assaulted.

Pause and reflect: Sexual boundary violations can be some of the most difficult experiences, leaving lasting emotional and psychological impacts. Consider how these violations have affected your relationship with your body and your sense of sexual agency. Reflect on the importance of establishing and communicating clear sexual boundaries and seeking support to heal from past violations.

UNHELPFUL CONNECTIONS

Boundary violations can significantly distort how we see ourselves, leading to unhelpful conclusions about our identities, particularly in a world where queer and trans identities are often moralized, pathologized, or medicalized. When our defenses are in place, we might internalize these stories without fully examining them, leading us to feel like there's something wrong or deficient about who we are. It's important to reflect on whether these stories and connections are genuinely serving us or reinforcing harmful beliefs.

Here are some examples of unhelpful connections you may have made:

1. **My queerness and transness are a result of abuse:** This belief may come from a desire to explain your identity in a way that aligns with harmful cultural narratives. However, queerness and transness are not "caused" by trauma or abuse. Your identity is not a reaction to harm but an authentic part of who you are.

2. **I have been made passive and feminized by the abuse of toxic masculinity:** Toxic masculinity can enforce rigid roles and expectations, but abuse does not determine your identity or behavior. You are not passive or feminized because of what you have endured; toxic masculinity itself is the problem, not you.

3. **I went to a sexualized space, so my discomfort with what occurred is completely on me:** Many queer spaces are sexualized, but this does not mean that any discomfort or violation is your fault. You have the right to establish boundaries and feel safe, no matter the environment. The responsibility for violations always lies with those who disrespect boundaries, not those who set them.

4. **I was drunk and high, so I guess what happened is partly my fault:** Substance use does not justify boundary violations or sexual assault. Consent must be enthusiastic, ongoing, and clear, regardless of the circumstances. Feeling incapacitated or disoriented does not make you responsible for someone else's violation of your boundaries.

5. **HIV was inevitable given my abuse history:** This belief may stem from internalized stigma surrounding HIV and queerness, but it's important to recognize that health outcomes are shaped by behaviors, environments, and systems—not a "destiny" tied to abuse.

According to psychologist Margaret Paul, self-blame represents a false sense of control as a response to shame. We may believe that if we were somehow at fault for a violation, we could have prevented it, giving us the illusion of control over what happened (2011). However, this is not true. Others' harmful behavior is not a reflection of your worth or actions. By releasing the attachment to control and understanding that you were not responsible for the violation, you can begin to heal from shame and blame.

Continue engaging in conversations with trusted individuals to explore and dismantle these unhelpful connections. Healing is a journey, and inviting others to support you in reframing your beliefs can be a powerful step.

EXERCISE: COGNITIVE RESTRUCTURING

Now that you've identified some boundary violations and reflected on their impact, it's time to challenge any unhelpful core beliefs that may have formed as a result. Cognitive restructuring is a technique used in cognitive behavioral therapy (CBT) to help individuals identify and challenge distorted thoughts and replace them with more balanced, realistic beliefs.

Let's look at two examples from the list above and connect them to potential unhelpful core beliefs:

1. **Example:** A nonbinary teen confides in a family member about their gender identity, only for that person to share it with others without permission.
    - **Unhelpful core belief:** "I can't trust anyone with my personal information."
    - **Cognitive restructuring:** It's understandable to feel hurt when someone betrays your trust, but that doesn't mean everyone is untrustworthy. Consider how you can establish clear boundaries and communicate your needs to others in the future.

2. **Example:** A bisexual man in his workplace is asked by his boss to talk about his personal life in front of coworkers.
    - **Unhelpful core belief:** "I have to share personal details to be accepted or valued at work."
    - **Cognitive restructuring:** Your value at work is not dependent on sharing personal information. It's important to maintain professional boundaries and feel empowered to decline requests that make you uncomfortable.

Core Beliefs

Take some time to identify an unhelpful core belief that may have resulted from a boundary violation you experienced. Write it down, and then challenge it using the cognitive restructuring technique. What is a more balanced, realistic belief that you can adopt? How does this new belief make you feel about yourself and your relationships?

With cognitive restructuring, you can begin to reshape how you view yourself, others, and the world, leading to healthier relationships and a stronger sense of self.

EMPTY CHAIR: A PERPETRATOR

This exercise is designed to help you express the unspoken thoughts, emotions, and questions you may have about someone who violated your boundaries. By engaging in this process, you'll have the opportunity to voice the impact the violation had on you, confront the person who harmed you, and reflect on how that conversation makes you feel.

Step 1: Create the Space

- Find a quiet and private space where you feel comfortable.

- Place two chairs facing each other—one chair represents you, and the other represents the person who violated your boundaries. You can imagine a specific scenario where a boundary was crossed, or you can think about a relevant general situation in your life.

- Take a few deep breaths, grounding yourself in the present moment. Know that this exercise is for you and your healing process, so there's no right or wrong way to do it.

Step 2: Speak to the Perpetrator

- Sit in the chair that represents you. Visualize the person who crossed your boundary sitting in the chair across from you. Imagine they are here, listening to you.

- Begin by telling them about the specific violation and how it impacted you. Here's a script you can use to guide your conversation:

"When you [describe the boundary violation], it made me feel [describe your emotions—e.g., disrespected, unsafe, powerless, angry, sad]. I have been carrying the weight of this experience with me, and it has affected how I see myself and my relationships. I didn't have the chance to fully express this to you at the time, but I need you to hear me now.

"I want to know—why did you do this? What were you thinking or feeling at the time? Did you even realize the harm you were causing?"

Step 3: Switch Chairs and Embody the Perpetrator

- Now, switch chairs. Sit in the seat of the perpetrator. As you sit down, take a moment to embody their perspective. Imagine what it might feel like for them to hear what you've just said. You don't need to justify their actions or make excuses for them—just imagine what emotions or thoughts might come up for them.

- If you feel comfortable, you can respond as the perpetrator. What do you think they would say in this moment? Would they feel remorse, denial, or defensiveness? What might they want to explain?

- Take a few moments to sit with the complexity of the situation, without needing to resolve it immediately.

Step 4: Conclusion

- After sitting in the perpetrator's chair, return to your original seat.

- Take a moment to reflect on how it felt to confront this person, even if they didn't respond the way you wanted them to. You've now voiced something that may have been unspoken for a long time, and that is a powerful step toward healing.

FINAL REFLECTIONS

- How did it feel to express your pain and ask the perpetrator why they did what they did?

- Did you gain any insight from imagining their response?

- Do you feel like the perpetrator was able to hear and receive what you had to say?

- What emotions are you left with? Do you feel more closure, or is there still work to be done?

Part 3

YOUR HEALTH

Chapter 12

ACCESSING MEDICAL CARE

When we think about our health, it's easy to focus on physical well-being—exercise, nutrition, maybe managing chronic conditions. But for many gay, bi, queer, and trans men, accessing healthcare isn't just about a physical check-up—it's about ensuring their identity is respected, understood, and affirmed. Why does that matter for mental health? Because affirming healthcare isn't just "nice-to-have"—it's a crucial aspect of holistic well-being.

Imagine going to a healthcare provider who assumes you're straight or doesn't understand what "queer" or "nonbinary" means. For many of us, this is a reality that leads to anxiety, stress, and ultimately, avoidance of care. Studies show that when healthcare providers lack cultural competence or reinforce heteronormative assumptions, it creates real barriers to care, leading many LGBTQ+ individuals to feel invisible, misunderstood, or outright disrespected (Haines et al. 2021; Kleinhans 2019).

When you don't feel seen, heard, or respected, it can affect your mental health just as much as your physical health. Conversely, an affirming healthcare experience can reduce anxiety, increase trust, and improve health outcomes by addressing both mental and physical aspects of well-being (Hickey et al. 2023). Access to competent and inclusive care means you're not only getting medical attention—you're also affirming your identity, which is an act of self-care.

AWARENESS EXERCISE

Reflect on your experiences in healthcare settings. Have you ever encountered the presumption of heterosexuality? Perhaps you've had to correct a provider who incorrectly assumed your partner's gender or avoided bringing up your sexual orientation for fear of judgment.

Use the following prompts to explore how these experiences have affected your approach to healthcare:

1. **Recall a time when you visited a healthcare provider:** Did they ask about your sexual orientation, or did they make assumptions? How did this make you feel about discussing your health openly?

2. **Consider your last few medical appointments:** Did you avoid disclosing your identity or relevant details about your personal life? What fears or concerns came up for you when thinking about how your provider might react?

3. **How does the presumption of hetero-sexuality affect your trust in healthcare providers?** Would you feel more comfortable if they asked open-ended questions about your identity and health needs?

As you reflect, remember: affirming care isn't a privilege—it's your right. It's essential to recognize these subtle (or sometimes overt) messages and how they shape your mental and physical health experiences.

COMMON BARRIERS

Navigating healthcare as a GBTQ guy often involves multiple layers of stigma, discrimination, and misinformation. These experiences can significantly impact mental health and overall well-being. Let's discuss some of the most common barriers to accessing competent, affirming care.

Discrimination and stigma in healthcare settings: Research consistently shows that many LGBTQ+ individuals delay or avoid seeking healthcare due to fears of discrimination or past negative experiences (Alba et al. 2020; Kleinhans 2019). These experiences aren't just one-off moments—they can profoundly affect how often someone seeks care, or whether they seek it at all.

Healthcare stereotype threat: Another barrier that adds to the anxiety is healthcare stereotype threat. Healthcare stereotype threat refers to the fear or expectation of being treated in a discriminatory way based on your identity (Saunders et al. 2023). For example, a gay man may fear that a provider will assume his health issues are related to his sexuality, while a trans man might worry about being misgendered or questioned about his transition. These feelings create a psychological burden that can manifest as avoidance—canceling appointments or withholding personal health information.

Institutional distrust: Marginalized communities, especially those with a history of criminal justice involvement, often experience a deep distrust of healthcare institutions. For many gay and bi men, particularly those from communities of color or with low socioeconomic status, this distrust can act as a significant barrier to preventive care like HIV pre-exposure prophylaxis (PrEP) (Peterson et al. 2018). Concerns about confidentiality, discrimination, and being treated poorly fuel this distrust and avoidance of crucial healthcare services.

Lack of provider knowledge: Even when a person feels safe enough to seek care, they may encounter providers who lack the cultural competency to understand their health needs. Many healthcare providers are not adequately trained on LGBTQ+ health issues, which can lead to dismissive or inappropriate care (Haines et al. 2021). Whether it's inaccurate information about hormone therapy for trans men or a lack of guidance on safer sex practices, this knowledge gap contributes to a healthcare system that doesn't fully serve the needs of LGBTQ+ individuals.

AWARENESS EXERCISE: STEREOTYPE THREAT AND ANXIETY

When it comes to accessing healthcare, fears about being judged or stereotyped can create significant barriers for GBTQ men. This anxiety can make it difficult to speak openly with providers, or even prevent you from seeking care altogether.

Take a moment to reflect on your own healthcare experiences:

- **When was the last time I avoided seeking healthcare due to fear of being judged?**

    Think about a time when you delayed or skipped a doctor's appointment. What specific concerns or fears did you have about the interaction?

- **What assumptions do I believe healthcare providers may have about me based on my sexuality or gender identity?**

  Consider how these assumptions may have influenced the care you received or how openly you communicated with your provider.

By reflecting on these experiences, you can start to identify how stereotype threat may have impacted your health decisions and what steps you can take to advocate for yourself moving forward.

THOUGHT ANALYSIS

Often, our thoughts around healthcare interactions are shaped by past experiences or fears about discrimination. While these thoughts may feel valid, they can also limit our ability to seek care and build trust with providers. Let's work through some unhelpful thoughts and find more balanced alternatives.

1. **Situation:** You've scheduled a doctor's appointment, but you're feeling anxious about how the provider might treat you once they learn about your sexual orientation or gender identity.

2. **Feelings and behaviors:** Anxiety, fear of judgment, feeling tense or guarded. You may avoid sharing personal health details.

3. **Prominent unhelpful thought:** "They won't understand my needs or take me seriously because I'm queer."

4. **Evaluate:** What evidence do you have that this thought is true? Have there been times when providers were respectful? Could it be that some providers lack education but are still willing to help? What are your options if you feel dismissed?

5. **Balanced alternative thought:** "Some providers may not fully understand LGBTQ+ issues, but I can find those who are affirming and advocate for myself. I deserve respectful and competent care."

By shifting these unhelpful thoughts into more balanced ones, you empower yourself to seek the care you need and advocate for better healthcare experiences.

KEY CONVERSATIONS

When it comes to accessing healthcare, it's essential to advocate for yourself and have open conversations with your provider about your unique needs. These conversations can be tough, especially when you've had negative experiences in the past. But they are key to receiving affirming care that addresses your full health—physical, mental, and sexual. Here are a few key topics to bring up with your healthcare provider:

- **Exploring sexual orientation and gender identity:** It's crucial to create a safe space for yourself to discuss any questions or uncertainties about your sexual orientation or gender identity. Normalize these conversations with your healthcare provider to ensure they understand your identity and can offer appropriate care. The more open you can be, the more your provider will understand how to tailor their advice and treatment options.

- **Safer sex and harm reduction information:** When it comes to sexual health, specific, nonjudgmental advice is essential. Your healthcare provider should give you clear guidance on safer sex practices, including condom use, PrEP, and harm reduction strategies related to substance use. If you feel your provider is not offering the advice you need, it's okay to seek out someone who will take your health concerns seriously (McCann et al. 2020).

- **Access to PrEP and PEP:** If you're at higher risk for HIV, it's important to discuss pre-exposure prophylaxis (PrEP) and post-exposure prophylaxis (PEP) with your provider. These are powerful prevention tools, but you should also ask about side effects, accessibility, and long-term care options (Ayala and Spieldenner 2021). Ensuring you have accurate and up-to-date information on these medications can significantly improve your sexual health.

- **HIV/STI testing and treatment infor-mation:** Regular HIV and STI (sexually transmitted infection) testing is a cornerstone of sexual health. Your provider should guide you on how often to get tested and what steps to take if an infection is detected. If you're on HIV treatment, medication adherence is critical, and discussing any challenges you have with adherence can lead to better support and care.

- **Hormone replacement therapy (HRT) and gender-affirming care:** For trans men, conversations about hormone replacement therapy (HRT) are crucial. Ask your provider about endocrinology assessments, the effects of hormones on your body, and what realistic expectations you should have (Sell and Krims 2021). Understanding the impact of HRT and getting clear guidance on your journey is key to feeling confident in your choices.

- **Surgical consultations—costs, risks, and benefits:** If you're considering gender-affirming surgery, it's important to talk openly about the costs, risks, and benefits. Surgical consultations are an opportunity to explore your options, ask detailed questions, and get a clear picture of what the process involves. Ask your provider about the recovery process, long-term outcomes, and any risks associated with surgery.

- **Mental health is health:** And it's an essential part of your overall well-being. Many GBTQ men face unique challenges that can impact their mental health. For example, bisexual individuals often feel invisible in both LGBTQ+ and straight communities, which can exacerbate feelings of isolation or contribute to mental health struggles (McCann et al. 2020). It's important to find mental health providers who understand the specific challenges you face. Look for affirming providers who are knowledgeable about LGBTQ+ issues and can offer culturally competent care. Your mental health is just as important as your physical health, and seeking out a provider who "gets it" is a crucial step in your healthcare journey.

If you feel any of these areas are lacking, it might be time to have a conversation with your provider or seek out a healthcare professional who is more attuned to your needs.

FINAL REFLECTIONS

Taking control of your healthcare journey is about more than just scheduling appointments—it's about advocating for your needs, ensuring you receive affirming care, and addressing any gaps in your health services. Here are some reflection questions to guide you as you take charge of your healthcare:

- What steps can I take to find healthcare providers who are affirming and culturally competent?
- How can I advocate for myself when discussing my sexual orientation, gender identity, or health needs with a provider?
- What fears or anxieties do I have about accessing care, and how can I challenge those fears?
- How can I better integrate mental health care into my overall well-being plan?

You deserve care that is respectful, knowledgeable, and attuned to your needs. Whether it's finding the right provider or asking the right questions, taking control of your healthcare is a vital part of ensuring long-term mental and physical health.

Chapter 13

SEXUAL HEALTH

Sexual health is a significant aspect of overall well-being, particularly for GBTQ individuals, whose experiences, education, and cultural narratives around sexual health can deeply influence their mental health. The information we absorb from sexual health education, early STI testing, and the way our society talks about sexual health often leaves its mark. For many GBTQ guys, sexual health discussions are inseparable from the stigma and moral panic around HIV and STIs. Even within our own community, the language around sexual health—like asking if someone is "clean"—reflects this internalized stigma.

We might not realize how much these concerns impact our mental health—how we feel about ourselves, our bodies, and the world around us. Navigating sexual health as a GBTQ person means moving through a world that still equates being gay with risk and disease. Let's explore the legacy of AIDS, the lingering anxieties many of us face today, and how these narratives shape our mental and emotional well-being.

LEGACY OF AIDS

The AIDS epidemic (beginning in the 1980s, peaking in 2004, and continuing through today) left a profound and lasting impact on older GBTQ men, many of whom lived through the height of the crisis. For them, the epidemic may have resulted in "survivor's guilt"—an emotional response to having lived while many others didn't. This generation may feel a deep, lingering grief, especially as they mourn not only the loss of loved ones but also the sense of community and activism that arose during that time. Many older men find themselves isolated in the present day, struggling with the loss of a generation of peers who once shared their lives and experiences.

For younger GBTQ men, the AIDS epidemic is more of a distant historical event. However, they haven't been untouched by it. For many, coming out as gay was immediately met with conversations or warnings about HIV, linking their identity to awareness of health risks. This generational anxiety around sexual health—especially through the lens of hookup apps where conversations around HIV status and PrEP are common—creates a landscape where sexual health is at the forefront long before it is for straight counterparts. The stigma may be less visible, but it's no less potent.

AWARENESS EXERCISE

Take a moment to reflect on how sexual health has shaped your mental well-being. Consider the following questions:

1. **What messages about sexual health did you receive when you first came out?**

    Were you immediately warned about HIV and STIs? How did those messages make you feel about yourself and your sexuality?

2. **How do conversations around sexual health impact your self-esteem?**

    When discussing HIV status, PrEP, or STIs with potential partners, how do you feel? Does it affect how you see yourself or your desirability?

3. **What emotions come up when you think about the legacy of AIDS?**

    Do you feel disconnected from older generations, or do you find yourself carrying any of the grief or fear they experienced? How does this affect your sense of belonging in the GBTQ community?

PERSPECTIVES ON STIS AND WELLNESS

Sexual health is not just about physical well-being; it's also deeply tied to how we view ourselves, our relationships, and our sense of safety in the world. For GBTQ guys, navigating the landscape of STIs often involves heightened anxiety, fear, and sometimes even shame. This is especially true in situations where there is a perceived risk—even if that risk is low.

Let's consider the case of Syed, a GBTQ man living in Atlanta. After a casual encounter following a night at the bar, Syed woke up the next day riddled with anxiety. Even though the encounter was low-risk, he couldn't shake the feeling that something was wrong. The more he replayed the night in his head, the more convinced he became that he might have contracted HIV. This spiral of worry led Syed to spend the entire day online, looking up symptoms and checking his body for any signs of infection.

This experience is common among many GBTQ men and is part of what's known as *symbolic interactionism*—a theory that suggests we rewrite past events to fit our current emotional states. In Syed's case, his anxiety rewrote the low-risk encounter as something far more dangerous, convincing him that he was likely HIV positive. This kind of worry often stems from a mix of internalized homophobia, societal stigma, and a desire for closure, even if that closure is negative (Barasz and Hagerty 2021).

COMMON AUTOMATIC THOUGHTS

When anxiety about STIs or HIV exposure kicks in, several common automatic thoughts might accompany that fear. These thoughts can affect your mental health and shape how you feel about yourself and your sexual experiences. Here are some common automatic thoughts that might spring up.

1. **Punishment:** *I did a bad thing.*

You might feel like you deserve to be punished for having sex, especially if there's any shame associated with the encounter.

2. **Shame:** *It wasn't worth it.*

This thought reflects regret and the internalized belief that pleasure or desire should be met with guilt.

3. **Self-criticism:** *I wasn't careful enough.*

Even in low-risk situations, you may feel that you didn't take enough precautions, leading to self-blame and anxiety.

4. **Acceptance:** *It's annoying but inevitable.*

This thought reflects a resignation that getting an STI is just part of being sexually active, which can dull your sense of agency over your health.

MORAL PANIC

Moral panic refers to the intense, widespread fear or anxiety that certain behaviors or identities—often minority identities—pose a significant threat to societal norms. For GBTQ men, moral panic around sexual health, particularly HIV and STIs, has historically contributed to damaging stereotypes, shame, and discrimination. These societal pressures have a profound effect on mental health, influencing how we see ourselves and how others perceive us.

For decades, GBTQ men have been subjected to societal fears that equate being gay with disease. The AIDS epidemic only amplified this, leading to an association between gay identity and illness that still lingers (Epstein 1992). Even as medical advancements like PrEP and undetectable = untransmittable (U=U) have made HIV more manageable, the stigma remains. This moral panic contributes to internalized shame and fear, often causing GBTQ men to feel isolated, misunderstood, or even unworthy of love and intimacy.

THOUGHT ANALYSIS: STI SYMPTOMS

Let's break down your thoughts and feelings about a potential STI symptom using a CBT thought analysis exercise. This will help you manage your anxiety and gain perspective.

1. **Situation:** I noticed green discharge while I was masturbating.

2. **Feelings and behaviors:** Anxiety, fear of having contracted an STI, obsessively checking for more symptoms, and avoiding sexual activity. Disgust with symptoms.

3. **Prominent unhelpful thought:** "I must have an STI because I wasn't careful enough, and now I'm going to suffer long-term consequences. It might even be HIV!"

4. **Evaluate:** Is this about being cautious, or is it bad luck? Are STIs a form of punishment, or am I making a choice to punish myself?

5. **Balanced alternative thought:** "I haven't done anything wrong, though this experience is quite unpleasant. This can likely be fixed with antibiotics. Discharge is not a symptom of HIV. It's normal to be anxious about testing, and sometimes bodies just do gross things!"

Let's return to Syed's story. After his low-risk encounter, Syed spiraled into anxiety, convinced that he had contracted HIV. This hypervigilance about health is a common reaction to the moral panic many GBTQ men have internalized. Syed's experience highlights the psychological toll that this fear takes, often leaving us feeling disconnected from our bodies, our pleasure, and our sense of safety in relationships.

By understanding the roots of this anxiety—internalized stigma, societal pressures, and moral panic—you can begin to break free from it. Recognizing that these fears are not reflections of your actual health status or worth, but rather products of societal narratives, is the first step in reclaiming your mental and sexual well-being.

LIVING WELL WITH HIV

Living with HIV, whether recently diagnosed or as a long-term survivor, can significantly impact mental health and overall well-being. For many GBTQ men, managing HIV isn't just about physical health—it's also about navigating the emotional, social, and psychological challenges that come with the diagnosis. Understanding the context of seroconversion, the support available, and the stigma that persists is crucial for maintaining mental wellness.

CONTEXT OF SEROCONVERSION

For many, the experience of seroconversion—the point at which you become HIV positive—can be overwhelming. It's often accompanied by a flood of emotions, including fear, shame, and confusion. You might immediately start questioning what your diagnosis means for your relationships, your sexual life, and your future. This initial reaction is deeply influenced by societal stigma and the internalized narratives many of us have grown up with around HIV (Amato and Émond 2023).

MEANINGS OF INFECTION

The way you interpret your HIV diagnosis—what it means for your life, your relationships, and your future—can shape your mental health. Some might view it as a moral or personal failure. Others might interpret it as a challenge to be managed, integrating it into their lives without letting it define them. The narrative you construct around your diagnosis can either empower you or deepen feelings of stigma and isolation. Of course, if you've attached negative meaning to being HIV positive, that is not just on you, having likely originated in societal stigma.

STIGMA

HIV stigma remains pervasive, both in the outside world and, unfortunately, within the GBTQ community. Many HIV-positive men worry about disclosing their status to potential partners, fearing rejection or judgment. This stigma not only impacts relationships, but can also affect self-esteem and beliefs about your worth and desirability. The criminalization of not telling partners that you're HIV positive in some places further complicates this, creating fear and anxiety around dating and intimacy (Amato and Émond 2023).

SELF-CONCEPT

Many people living with HIV struggle with the idea that they could be seen as a "vector of illness"—someone who poses a risk to others. Even with medical advancements like undetectable = untransmittable (U=U), this perception can weigh heavily on mental health. It can lead to feelings of guilt, fear, or anxiety about intimate relationships, especially if your partner doesn't fully understand the science behind HIV transmission. Releasing this fear and embracing the truth that people living with HIV can live full, healthy, and loving lives is a critical part of wellness.

ADEQUATE SUPPORT

One of the key factors that determine how well someone adapts to living with HIV is the support system they have in place. Adequate social, medical, and emotional support can make a world of difference. Having friends, family, or community members who offer nonjudgmental support can alleviate feelings of isolation. Access to a knowledgeable healthcare provider who understands both the physical and emotional aspects of living with HIV is equally important. Support groups and online communities can also offer a space to connect with others who understand what you're going through.

THOUGHT ANALYSIS: DISCLOSING HIV STATUS

Let's break down your thoughts and feelings about disclosing your HIV status to help you manage any fears or anxiety around it.

1. **Situation:** I had a great first date last night, and I was going to share that I'm HIV positive, but decided not to.

2. **Feelings and behaviors:** Anxiety, fear of rejection, guilt about not disclosing, and hesitation about a second date.

3. **Prominent unhelpful thought:** "If I tell him I'm HIV positive, he'll lose interest, and I'll never find a partner."

4. **Evaluate:** Is it true that disclosing my status will automatically result in rejection? Have I seen evidence that people will always react negatively, or could this be based on fear or stigma?

5. **Balanced alternative thought:** "Not everyone will reject me for being HIV positive. It's better to share my status when I feel ready, and if the person truly values me, they'll take the time to understand and support me."

By evaluating your thoughts in this way, you can reduce the anxiety around disclosure and approach it with more confidence and self-compassion.

EMPTY CHAIR: FEAR VS. LONGING

This exercise is designed to help you explore the internal conflict between *Fear* and *Longing* in the context of your sexual health, connection, and desire. It's common for fear—often stemming from societal stigma around STIs and the legacy of HIV/AIDS—to coexist with longing, your natural human desire for pleasure and intimacy.

As you work through this exercise, you'll have the opportunity to engage in a dialogue between these two parts of yourself: fear and longing. This will help you normalize pleasure as a right, see connection and desire as natural, and understand that STIs are just a normal part of life, not something to be stigmatized.

Step 1: Create the Space

- Set up two chairs. One represents Fear and the other represents Longing.
- Make sure you're comfortable and that the space is quiet, where you can focus without distractions.

Step 2: Start with Fear

- Sit in the chair or spot that represents Fear. Imagine that this part of you is sitting across from you.
- Take a deep breath. Now, start talking to Fear. Ask it questions and listen for the answers.
- You might say: "Fear, I see you. You're worried about intimacy, STIs, and rejection. You've learned from the world that sexual pleasure and connection are risky. Why do you feel this way?"
- Speak from your heart. Let your fears surface, however big or small they are. There's no judgment here—this is your space to explore.

Step 3: Switch to Longing

- Now, stand up and move to the chair representing Longing. Here, your desire for intimacy and connection sits. Imagine yourself fully in this role of longing and allow it to speak.

- What does your longing want to say? You might say: "Longing, I feel you. You want to experience connection, love, and pleasure without fear. You believe that pleasure is a natural part of life. Tell me more about what you need."

- Let your longing express itself freely. What do you desire? What would your sexual and emotional life look like without fear holding you back?

Step 4: Switch Back to Fear

- Move back to the chair of Fear and respond. Let Fear explain its concerns further.

- It might say: "I'm scared of getting hurt. I'm scared of rejection or getting an STI. The world has told me that being sexually active comes with risks, and I want to protect you."

- Be open to hearing what Fear has to say. Acknowledge that it's trying to keep you safe, even though it might be holding you back.

Step 5: Return to Longing

- Move again to the chair of Longing. Let it express how it feels about Fear's concerns.

- Maybe it says: "I hear you, Fear, but I want to experience love, connection, and pleasure. I know there are risks, but that doesn't mean I should deny myself the joy of intimacy. I believe STIs are just a part of life, and with care and communication, I can manage them. I want to experience pleasure without shame."

- Allow your longing to respond honestly and fully.

Step 6: Conclusion

- Continue this back-and-forth conversation as many times as you need. Each time, try to get a little deeper into the dialogue.
- When you feel finished, take a deep breath, and return to the present moment.

FINAL REFLECTIONS

- What would it look like to embrace intimacy and pleasure while also acknowledging your fears but not letting them control you?
- How can you honor both parts of yourself in a way that feels balanced and safe?
- What did you learn from hearing both Fear and Longing speak?
- Does this change the way you think about your sexual health, your relationships, and your desires? How so?

Chapter 14

SUBSTANCE USE

When we talk about substance use, it's important to recognize that for many GBTQ people, drugs and alcohol serve multiple roles in their lives. Whether in social settings, to enhance sexual experiences, to self-medicate for chronic pain or illness, or as a way of coping with stress and trauma, substances can be both a part of our collective identity and a challenge to navigate. Studies have shown that GBTQ folks, especially gay and bisexual men, are more likely to engage in substance use than their heterosexual peers (McGuire et al. 2020; Gebru et al. 2023).

Substance use can often be tied to the need for belonging and acceptance within our communities. For example, The Crystal Methamphetamine Project found that many gay, bi, and queer men used crystal meth to enhance sexual experiences, reduce inhibitions, and foster connections with others in sexual and social contexts (McGuire et al. 2020). For some, substances become a way to connect with peers in party scenes like "party n' play" (PnP), while for others, drugs and alcohol help alleviate the pain of rejection, discrimination, or past trauma (Gebru et al. 2023; Batchelder et al. 2021).

It's important to approach the topic of substances with curiosity and compassion, recognizing that for many GBTQ folks, these choices are deeply interwoven with their experiences of the world. Understanding the complexities of why we use substances can be the first step in assessing whether these behaviors are serving us or causing harm.

AWARENESS EXERCISE

Reflect on the role substances play in your life. When do you find yourself using drugs or alcohol? Is it at parties, during sex, or when you're feeling stressed? Consider the reasons behind your choices. Are substances helping you connect with others, relax, or cope with difficult emotions?

Now think about your peer group. What are the norms around substance use? Do your friends or partners encourage drinking or using drugs in certain situations? For many GBTQ folks, substances are a part of the social fabric of the GBTQ communities, but it's important to reflect on your values and mental health (Moon et al. 2024). By becoming more aware of the personal and social functions of substance use, you can better understand its impact on your well-being.

DEFINING PROBLEMATIC USE

Substance use is often normalized in certain cultures and communities. In GBTQ spaces, especially party and club scenes, alcohol and drugs like crystal meth are sometimes seen as just part of the experience (McGuire et al. 2020; Gebru et al. 2023). Whether it's to celebrate, mourn, or simply socialize, using substances may feel like a normal part of life. But when does substance use cross the line from something that feels enjoyable to something that feels out of control?

The Centre for Addiction and Mental Health (CAMH) defines addiction using the "Four Cs"—craving, control, compulsion, and consequences (2018). Ask yourself the following:

1. Do you find yourself *craving* substances when you're not using them?
2. Are you struggling to *control* how much or how often you use?
3. Is using drugs or alcohol becoming something you feel compelled to do, even when it's not enjoyable? Or, do you radically reorganize your time and resources to optimize opportunities to use/party? These indicate *compulsion*.
4. Have you continued to use even when you know the *consequences* outweigh the benefits?

If you answered yes to these questions, consider reflecting on whether your substance use is becoming problematic. But remember, not every GBTQ person who uses substances has a problem. For some, setting harm reduction goals—like using safely or cutting back—can be more realistic than quitting altogether (CAMH 2018). For others, an abstinence-based approach may feel more in line with their goals.

No matter where you find yourself, the first step is recognizing that substance use is a personal journey, one that can be navigated with intention and care. Whether you're interested in harm reduction or exploring sobriety, there are resources available to help you make decisions that are right for you (Herie et al. 2006; Gebru et al. 2023).

At the same time, we find ourselves in the midst of an opioid crisis, which leads to unnecessary deaths. So, as a community, we need to be aware of harm reduction strategies such as naloxone kits and safer injection practices, because unintended outcomes in these circumstances are not related to frequency and quantity of use.

Case Scenario

Rahman, *a forty-year-old queer man living in Toronto, has always been the life of the party. His social life revolves around alcohol, and he finds comfort in the company of friends and his favorite drinks. Alcohol has always felt like a reliable companion to Rahman, enhancing every event and mood. However, as he begins to reflect on his relationship with alcohol, he is considering a harm reduction approach to cut back.*

Rahman's drinking has evolved into a daily habit. He drinks both alone and socially, with particularly heavy weekends involving not just alcohol but also cocaine. House parties, dance floors, and late-night escapades have long defined his weekends, but this lifestyle is starting to take a toll—financially and in overall well-being. After coming across Canada's Guidance on Alcohol and Health *(Paradis et al. 2023), which suggests that no amount of alcohol is entirely safe and that drinking more than two standard drinks per week can increase the risk of alcohol-related harm, Rahman has begun questioning his habits.*

Though Rahman wants to reduce his alcohol consumption, he fears what life without alcohol might mean. His social life has always revolved around drinking, and he worries that without alcohol, he won't be as sociable or engaging. Additionally, the idea of seeking or having sex while sober feels daunting, as he's always relied on alcohol to reduce his inhibitions in intimate situations.

DIGGING DEEPER: PART ONE

The following questions can help Rahman—and you—gain insight into the deeper emotional roots of substance use and how these habits may have developed over time. Take a moment to reflect on the following:

1. What role have bars and alcohol played in shaping your identity? How do substances help you express a part of yourself that might otherwise feel hidden or vulnerable?

2. How does alcohol influence your relationships? Do you find that substances bring you closer to others, or do they sometimes create distance or conflict? How might your relationships change if substances were less central?

3. What emotions do you rely on alcohol to soothe? Have you ever used substances to manage anxiety, loneliness, or other challenging emotions? What do you notice about the emotions that tend to arise when you don't have substances to lean on?

4. How has your relationship with alcohol or substances shifted over time? Are there moments when you've felt more in control or less in control of your use?

5. What fears arise when you think about reducing or eliminating alcohol from your life? What would you miss about substances if you chose to reduce or quit using them?

6. How do societal or cultural norms influence your substance use? In queer spaces, drinking and drug use can sometimes feel normalized, even expected. Have you ever felt pressure to use substances to fit in or be accepted? How might this social pressure affect your choices?

By reflecting on these questions, you can begin to understand the complex emotional layers that underpin substance use. Gaining insight into the unconscious motivations behind these habits can empower you to make more intentional choices about your relationship with substances moving forward.

SEXUALIZED SUBSTANCE USE

Sexualized substance use, commonly referred to as "chemsex" within GBTQ communities, involves the intentional use of drugs—such as crystal methamphetamine (crystal meth), GHB (gamma-hydroxybutyrate), and mephedrone—specifically to enhance sexual experiences. Chemsex typically occurs in group settings, often tied to a party or "party n' play" (PnP) culture, where the use of these substances can amplify feelings of pleasure, reduce inhibitions, and prolong sexual activity. While chemsex can offer a sense of freedom and euphoria for participants, it also carries significant risks and challenges.

According to *The Crystal Methamphetamine Project*, crystal meth use is particularly common in chemsex among gay, bi, and queer men. The project found that participants engaged in chemsex for three main reasons: to intensify sexual pleasure, to connect socially, and to cope with life stressors. Approximately 48 percent of respondents reported using meth to make sex more pleasurable, while another 48 percent used it to connect sexually with others (McGuire et al. 2020). Sexualized substance use has become integrated into social and sexual practices for some GBTQ individuals, offering not only physical satisfaction but also emotional fulfillment through intimacy and connection.

MOTIVATIONS BEHIND CHEMSEX

The motivations for engaging in chemsex are multifaceted and deeply connected to the unique challenges faced by GBTQ individuals. Studies suggest that sexualized substance use is often driven by a combination of sexual, social, and psychological factors. For many men, drugs like crystal meth help alleviate anxieties related to sexual performance, body image, and feelings of rejection (Gebru et al. 2023). Thus, chemsex can serve as a coping mechanism, offering a temporary escape from internalized homophobia, stigma, and societal pressures.

In addition to enhancing sexual pleasure, chemsex fosters a sense of belonging and social connection. In GBTQ spaces, where sex is often a defining element of identity, chemsex can create opportunities for intimacy and camaraderie, particularly for those who may feel marginalized in other areas of their lives. This sense of inclusion and validation is significant for many participants, as it allows them to feel connected in a community that may otherwise be difficult to access (McGuire et al. 2020; Card et al. 2019).

CHALLENGES AND RISKS

The biggest challenge with substances is often not the drug itself or the mechanism for consuming it, but rather the marginalized and moralized context in which they exist. For example, the ongoing drug policy crises across North America—the lack of willingness to decriminalize drugs and maintain barriers to effective harm reduction services—have led to many preventable deaths due to overdose.

If you are a GBTQ guy who uses recreational party drugs—whether paired with sexualized spaces or dancefloors—you may know the anxiety that comes with the reality that there aren't structural conditions in place to ensure you have a safe supply. Furthermore, if you've experienced a loss due to a drug overdose, you may feel a combination of grief and deep neglect from the communities you live in, including from other GBTQ folks. This is a profoundly isolating experience.

Witnessing preventable deaths due to overdose might act as a deterrent to drug use for some, but not for everyone. GBTQ guys in this subculture are at risk of internalizing social and political neglect from their environments, which leads to shame and low self-worth. This can be a trigger for more substance use, especially when paired with disenfranchised grief. If you are in the scene, it may be useful to reflect on how your relationship with substances has been affected by societal stigma and community responses to drug-related deaths.

As someone who parties, it's important to know what risks are associated with specific drugs and what circumstances are more likely to lead to an undesirable outcome. For example, the potential for overdose can be higher with GHB, which can be difficult to "dose" (i.e. measuring a safe quantity to take over a period of time). Another concern is the possibility of substances being laced with opioids (e.g., fentanyl) without the consumer being aware of it. Stimulants like cocaine and crystal meth are less likely to lead to an overdose but could trigger a dangerous cardiac event. In this context, harm reduction supplies and services, such as drug testing and overdose prevention kits (i.e. Naloxone), can be lifesaving.

Drug-related deaths are the worst-case scenarios. If you are part of the chemsex scene, you are acutely aware that many users struggle with social and psychological dependency. *The Crystal Methamphetamine Project* reported that a significant number of participants using crystal meth on a weekly basis felt addicted, with many acknowledging that while the drug initially made them feel more confident and connected, it ultimately resulted in feelings of isolation, guilt, and loss of control (McGuire et al. 2020).

Chemsex also increases the risk of sexually transmitted infections (STIs) and, for those who share needles, Hepatitis C (Batchelder et al. 2021). For people living with HIV, frequent substance use can interfere with treatment adherence and missed healthcare appointments. These facts shouldn't be used to drive fears around substances, but rather as a reminder to plan for regular testing and treatment, as well as ensuring access to needed harm reduction supplies. Remember that any physical health concerns will interact with your experiences of stress and mental well-being.

By recognizing the complexities behind chemsex, including its roots in trauma, social pressure, and the pursuit of pleasure, GBTQ men can make more informed decisions about their relationship with substances. Creating supportive environments where individuals can access mental health and addiction services without fear of judgment is essential in addressing the long-term consequences of chemsex in our communities.

Case Scenario

Omar, *a bisexual man in his late twenties, has seen his use of crystal meth increase over the past two years. What began as an occasional indulgence during online hookups has now become a weekly habit, driven by the drug's initial allure of intense pleasure and prolonged sexual encounters. Though Omar initially sought connection and desirability, his reliance on crystal meth has left him feeling more isolated than ever. He now finds himself confined to his apartment, struggling with the growing grip of addiction.*

Omar recognizes that his meth use is problematic, but seeking help has proven difficult. After a traumatic experience attending a support group, where he experienced auditory and visual hallucinations, his fear and isolation have only intensified. The same drug that once gave him a heightened sense of intimacy now exacerbates his mental health struggles. His hallucinations and deteriorating mental health suggest the possibility of a co-occurring mental health condition that requires urgent care.

DIGGING DEEPER: PART TWO

Omar's case highlights the complex relationship between substance use, sexual identity, and mental health. Reflecting on his experience and the following questions can offer valuable insight into how substances may influence not only sexual behaviors, but also deeper psychological needs.

1. How does substance use shape your sexual identity and imagination? Are there elements of your sexual self that feel more accessible when using substances, such as confidence or freedom from shame?

2. What role does fantasy play in your substance use? For many people, substances allow for the exploration of sexual fantasies that might feel

too vulnerable or inaccessible in sober situations. Have you noticed that substance use enhances your ability to engage with sexual fantasies or to push boundaries? How do you feel about these fantasies when you are not using substances?

3. What emotional needs are you trying to meet through substance use? Reflect on the emotions that arise before and after you use substances. What needs—whether for comfort, connection, or escape—are you trying to fulfill through your use of drugs or alcohol?

4. What fears do you have about what might happen to your sexual or emotional life if you cut back on substances? Are there parts of yourself that you feel would be harder to access or express without them?

5. How has substance use impacted your relationship with your body and sexuality? Do you feel more confident or detached from your physical sensations when using substances? What would it be like to engage in sexual experiences without relying on drugs or alcohol?

These questions invite deeper reflection on the ways substances can both facilitate and complicate access to sexual desires, fantasies, and identities. By understanding the underlying emotional and psychological needs driving substance use, you can begin to explore new pathways to intimacy and connection—ones that don't rely on the same patterns of behavior.

HARM REDUCTION EXERCISES

ABC ANALYSIS

The ABC model—Antecedent, Behavior, and Consequence—is a helpful way to analyze our patterns of substance use and can guide harm reduction strategies. You can explore what leads up to your use (antecedents), the behaviors associated with using, and the consequences that follow. Through this analysis, you can create intervention goals that allow for changes before, during, or after substance use.

Here's how you can apply ABC analysis as part of a harm reduction approach:

- **Example 1: Post-Work Stress**

    Antecedent: After a long and stressful day at work, I feel drained and want to unwind.

    Behavior: I pour myself a drink, which turns into four drinks, as I watch TV alone.

    Consequence: I feel temporarily relieved, but wake up the next morning feeling groggy and guilty for drinking so much.

    Intervention goal: I could plan to limit myself to one drink or replace drinking with another stress-relieving activity like taking a walk or calling a friend.

- **Example 2: Party Night**

    Antecedent: It's Friday night, and I'm feeling anxious about going to a party where I know everyone will be using GHB.

    Behavior: I decide to take GHB when I arrive at the party to ease my social anxiety and connect with others.

    Consequence: I feel more relaxed and social at the party, but I also blackout later in the night and wake up feeling disoriented.

    Intervention goal: Before the party, I could decide to limit my GHB use to one dose or plan for safer drug use (e.g., using with a trusted friend who can monitor).

- **Example 3: Isolation**

    Antecedent: I've been feeling isolated lately, and I'm scrolling through hookup apps where people are offering party drugs.

    Behavior: I engage in chemsex even though I told myself I'd cut back on crystal meth use.

    Consequence: After the high fades, I feel more isolated and anxious.

    Intervention goal: During the moment of feeling isolated, I could reach out to a friend or join a support group instead of partying. If I do decide to engage, I can set limits on my end time.

THOUGHT ANALYSIS: CRASH DAY

After a weekend of partying, it's common to experience a "crash," where feelings of depression, anxiety, and exhaustion set in. A thought analysis can help you navigate these moments by identifying unhelpful thoughts and replacing them with more balanced perspectives.

Here's a guided thought analysis for a "crash day":

1. **Situation:** It's Tuesday after a weekend of partying with GHB and MDMA, and I'm super depressed.

2. **Feelings and behaviors:** I feel exhausted, anxious, and overwhelmed. I'm isolating myself and avoiding my responsibilities.

3. **Prominent unhelpful thought:** "I'll never be able to get my life together. I'm just going to keep messing up."

4. **Evaluate:** This thought makes me feel hopeless and defeated. It's a common feeling after a crash, but it's also exaggerated and untrue. I have managed my life well in the past, even when I've struggled.

5. **Balanced alternative thought:** "This is a rough day, but I've gotten through tough times before. I can take small steps to feel better today, like eating something healthy and getting some rest."

Using these tools, you can gain greater awareness of your patterns, break down unhelpful thoughts, and set realistic harm reduction goals. These exercises empower you to make more intentional choices about substance use and its role in your life.

EMPTY CHAIR: THE HIGH

Sometimes, the substances we use—whether alcohol, weed, meth, or something else—feel like more than just substances. They feel like a state of being, like a version of ourselves that brings both excitement and anxiety. This exercise is designed to help you have a conversation with that high, and to unpack what it gives and takes.

In this Empty Chair exercise, you'll be speaking to your "high" or "inebriated" self, giving voice to both the appeal and the frustration it brings.

Step 1: Create the Space

- Find a quiet space where you can sit comfortably with an empty chair in front of you.

- Close your eyes for a moment and imagine that the version of yourself when you're high or intoxicated is sitting in the opposite chair.

- This is the part of you that craves the euphoria, relief, and confidence substances seem to provide. But it's also the part of you that can feel frustrated, disappointed, or even guilty when the high doesn't deliver what you want.

Step 2: Start the Conversation

Begin by speaking directly to your high, as if it were sitting right in front of you. Here are some prompts to get you started:

- **What do I like about you?**

    "When I'm high, I like that you make me feel confident, even sexy. You take away the worries I have about my body, about what people think of me. You make socializing easier and more fun. When I feel your buzz, the world feels lighter, and I feel like a better version of myself."

- **What anxieties do you bring?**

    "But at the same time, I'm always chasing you. I can't ever seem to get quite enough. I'm always worried that you won't show up the way I want. There are times when the high fades too soon, or it doesn't feel as good as I expected, and I feel let down. I keep thinking, 'What if this time, you let me down again?'"

- **What promises do you make me?**

    "You promise me confidence, that I'll be free from all my insecurities. You promise that I'll feel good, look better, be funnier, more interesting. I believe in you because you've given me those moments, fleeting as they are."

- **When do you disappoint me?**

    "But then there are the crashes. When the high fades, I'm left feeling more anxious, more alone than before. You leave me craving more, and I hate that. Sometimes, I feel like I'm constantly trying to live up to the promise of the high, and when you don't deliver, I feel frustrated. I thought you'd help me escape, but you leave me with more problems."

Step 3: Switch Seats and Speak as the High

Now, stand up and move to the empty chair. Sit down and imagine that *you* are the high. Speak as the high, responding to what you just said:

- **As the high:**

    "I know why you come to me. I'm seductive because I can offer you relief—relief from your fears, from insecurities about your body, from anxiety in social settings. I can make you feel invincible, at least for a little while. I let you push aside the things that hurt you; the things you want to forget."

- **Acknowledging guilt:**

    "But I also know I don't always keep my promises. Sometimes, I lure you in with the idea of pleasure, but I can be misleading. I know that I cause you pain and guilt when I wear off. I leave you disappointed, anxious, or isolated. I hate to admit it, but I'm not always what you need, and I often leave you worse off than before."

Final Reflections

- What do you notice about how you feel when you speak to your high?
- What has this conversation revealed about your relationship to substances?
- What would it look like to change this relationship?

By externalizing your high and having a direct conversation with it, you can start to unpack the layers of what you like about being high and what you dislike. The goal isn't necessarily to reach a conclusion right now, but to open up space for more intentional reflection. What you choose to do next is entirely up to you—but now, you're doing it with greater awareness.

Chapter 15

AGING

Aging is a journey we all take, but it's one that many of us would prefer to avoid thinking about. Whether it's the annual joke about how we're still thirty-five or the desire to maintain youthful energy and looks, the idea of getting older can feel threatening. This is particularly true in cultures influenced by Western Europe and the United States, where aging often goes uncelebrated, unlike some Global South cultures that honor their elders for their wisdom and life experience. As a result, our society sets us up for existential and identity crises as we age.

For GBTQ men, these pressures are compounded. Our communities can sometimes glorify youthfulness so much that aging becomes something to fear. One reason for this might be the trauma associated with the HIV/AIDS epidemic, which claimed so many lives and left behind a lingering association between illness and aging.

Further complicating things is the idea of resisting heteronormative milestones. Whether by choice or circumstance, many queer men haven't followed the conventional path of marriage, children, and settling down. This can leave us feeling isolated as we get older, without the "insurance policies" that intergenerational families provide. But getting older, like every part of life, can be a time of growth and new experiences—if we let it.

AWARENESS EXERCISE

Take a moment to reflect on how often you encounter the subtle or explicit message that being younger is better. This might be from media, social interactions, or even self-talk. How many times a week do you feel like you're being told—or telling yourself—that youth equals value?

Now, ask yourself: How much have I internalized these messages? Think about the ways this belief might show up in your own thinking, actions, and self-perception. Write down any examples that come to mind. The goal here is not to judge yourself, but to gain awareness of how pervasive these messages are and how much they influence your thoughts about aging.

INTERNALIZING AGEISM

Internalized ageism refers to the subtle but powerful ways in which we absorb and adopt society's negative views on aging, often without realizing it. We start to believe that aging is something to be feared or avoided, and we may begin to discriminate against ourselves. According to research, internalized ageism can have profound effects on our mental and physical health, contributing to lower self-esteem, higher stress levels, and even a reduced lifespan (Levy 2022).

A concrete example of internalized ageism might be saying, "I'm too old to start a new career," or feeling self-conscious about gray hairs. It could also look like avoiding social activities because you think you'll be the "old person" in the room. The danger of internalized ageism is that it can limit your behavior and your opportunities—whether it's deciding not to pursue new hobbies, date, or learn new skills (Scherrer and Dinman 2023). And in some cases, we might even start to believe we deserve less respect, care, or attention as we age.

BRIEF JOURNAL ENTRY

Take a few moments to journal about your thoughts and feelings around aging. What are your biggest fears about getting older? Here are a few prompts to help you explore this further:

- What does aging mean to me?
- What am I most afraid of as I get older?
- Do I feel pressure to stay young, and where does that pressure come from?

Now, consider: How can I challenge or confront these fears? Some prompts for reflection:

- What are some positive things about getting older that I haven't considered before?
- How can I start to embrace aging rather than fear it?
- Who in my life can serve as a positive example of aging with grace?

GBTQ AGING

In queer culture, we've all heard the joke about "gay death at 30" (Koziol 2015). The idea is that after thirty, gay men become invisible, no longer attractive or valued. But what is the impact of this harmful stereotype? For many, it reinforces a deep sense of insecurity and anxiety about aging. We internalize the message that to be older is to be less valuable, which can take a toll on our mental health and well-being.

Yet aging doesn't have to be something we dread. In fact, many older GBTQ individuals report finding a sense of stability, confidence, and self-awareness as they grow older (Cheves 2022). Research shows that with age comes resilience—many older queer individuals find themselves healthier, more at peace with their identities, and more connected to their communities than when they were younger (Batista and Pereira 2020).

However, there are still challenges. Aging in the queer community can feel isolating, especially if we lack the traditional support of family or long-term partners. The pressure to remain youthful and fit is also exacerbated by a community that sometimes seems to prize physical appearance above all else (Levy 2022). It's important to recognize these pressures, but also to push back against them, seeking out connections with others who embrace aging and view it as an opportunity for growth.

THOUGHT ANALYSIS: THINKING ABOUT BEING ALONE

Whether people are partnered or single, to some degree, we all die alone. This thought is terrifying for many people, let alone GBTQ guys. Fear of loneliness or the absence of someone to care for us in our elder years is a common concern. If this resonates with you, let's work through it using the thought analysis below.

1. **Situation:** I'm at a sixty-fifth birthday party, and many people have partners. I'm reminded of my age and singleness.
2. **Feelings and behaviors:** Feeling anxious, sad, and isolated. Withdrawing, avoiding conversation about my future. Feeling a sense of longing and fear for what might come as I grow older.
3. **Prominent unhelpful thought:** "I'll be elderly and frail with no one to look after me. One fall and I'll be in the ER and then my deathbed—all alone."
4. **Evaluate:** What evidence do I have that I will be all alone? Have I ever been in situations where I felt similarly, and things turned out better than expected? What support do I have now, even if I don't have a romantic partner? What steps can I take to build a supportive network for the future?
5. **Balanced alternative thought:** "I can't predict the future, but I know I am capable of building meaningful connections with friends, chosen family, and community. As I grow older, I can continue to create a life surrounded by people who care for and support me."

GRIEF AND GRATITUDE

GBTQ men often experience different life trajectories compared to their straight counterparts. It's normal to reflect and feel a mix of regret, grief, nostalgia, and gratitude. Straight or queer, everyone has their own share of life choices and missed opportunities, but it's essential not to compare your grief with others'. When it comes to nostalgia, research shows it can have a restorative function. Nostalgia helps us remember moments that matter, fostering a sense of connection to our past while also offering a sense of hope for the future (Zhou et al. 2008).

Case Scenario

Zavaré grew up in Singapore, where societal disapproval of queerness made him feel stifled. Upon completing his education, he moved to Minneapolis, where he could embrace his identity and career more freely. Now seventy, Zavaré occasionally wishes he had laid down roots and pursued long-term relationships or even had kids, but the trade-off was a rich life filled with adventure and new experiences.

His straight best friend, Amit, feels a different kind of longing. Amit, who settled down early and started a family, sometimes wishes he had taken time to have more experiences like Zavaré. Over coffee, they discuss how both of their choices brought deep satisfaction but also left them with occasional "what-ifs." They both realize that their respective paths brought different joys, but also that grief and gratitude go hand-in-hand. They honor what they've done and let go of what might have been.

Digging Deeper

To explore your personal relationship with grief, regret, and gratitude, consider the following questions:

1. What decisions have I made in life that I sometimes regret? What do those regrets tell me about my values or desires?

2. How does nostalgia show up for me? Do I view it as a positive reflection of my past, or does it feel bittersweet?

3. What are the things I'm most grateful for in my life, and how have they shaped my identity and experiences as a GBTQ person?

4. How can I practice acceptance and peace with the paths I didn't take, while still honoring the choices that brought me joy?

THE EMPTY CHAIR: YOUR OLDER SELF

In this exercise, you're going to use the Gestalt Empty Chair technique to have a conversation with your older self.

Step 1: Create the Space

- Set up two chairs somewhere quiet, where you will not be disturbed.

- Imagine sitting across from an older version of yourself—someone in their seventies, eighties, or beyond. This is the part of you that has witnessed so many changes and gained a wealth of life experience.

Step 2: Speak to Your Older Self

- Start by sitting in the chair as your current self.
- Begin with an apology to your older self for any ways you've allowed internalized ageism to hold you back—maybe by disconnecting from others, avoiding new experiences, or judging yourself harshly for aging.

Step 3: Speak to Your Present Self

- Now, switch chairs.
- As your older self, speak to your younger self. What advice would you give? How would you comfort or encourage your younger self to stay connected, engaged, and true to their wisdom?
- What commitments can you make to live a full and purposeful life as you age, to build connections and community, and to honor the years of wisdom you've accumulated?

FINAL REFLECTIONS

As you close this chapter, take a moment to reflect on the journey of aging.

- What are you most looking forward to as you get older?
- How can you start to challenge the unhelpful beliefs you've internalized about aging? Remember, getting older doesn't mean losing value—in fact, it often means gaining depth, insight, and resilience.
- How will you continue to nurture your sense of connection, purpose, and community as you grow into your older self?

CONCLUSION

Throughout this book, we've explored the many determinants of mental health for cis and trans queer guys—from the impacts of social context and family to relationships, health, and aging. We've covered topics such as managing the complex layers of coming out, handling rejection, healing body consciousness, and coping with disenfranchised grief. Techniques in this book were drawn from therapies like CBT, Gestalt, and psychodynamic methods, all designed to empower you with tools to understand, accept, and manage the factors affecting your mental well-being.

Depending on how you identify—whether as gay, bisexual, trans, nonbinary, queer, a combination of these, or something else in the universe of queer identities—your journey will have unique dimensions, and the experiences you face may look very different. For example, a bisexual person may explore which communities in our binary-dominant world feel most welcoming or may experience the erasure of their bisexual identity depending on the gender of their current partner. For someone who is trans or nonbinary, exclusion may show up in nuanced ways, like a lack of options on dating apps or the discomfort of navigating rigidly gendered spaces. If you're also a person of color, these experiences can be compounded by racial biases, creating layers of complexity in finding truly affirming spaces.

Regardless of how you identify, and especially if you're a gay man, the impact of heteronormativity might present itself in subtle yet powerful ways, like the pressure to conform to conventional milestones around relationships, marriage, or family. These milestones can often feel like they don't quite fit, leading to a journey of redefining success and fulfillment outside of societal norms. A queer person may feel pulled between various LGBTQ+ communities, sometimes facing judgment or exclusion even within queer spaces if they don't fit certain expectations around appearance, behavior, or labels.

These examples highlight how each identity brings its own set of challenges, resilience, and ways of navigating the world. And while these experiences differ, they also intersect, shaping a landscape of belonging, rejection, visibility, and connection that is constantly evolving. This book honors those differences and aims to provide tools for healing, resilience, and personal growth across the spectrum of queer experiences.

We are all in these communities and on these journeys together, even as they may feel difficult and isolating. When things get tough, I urge you to remember this: you are not alone. Our community is a beautiful, rainbow-colored tapestry of individuals and experiences, and no matter who you are, you deserve community, healing, and joy. I truly hope this book has helped you get there.

To deepen your journey, visit http://www.newharbinger.com/55039 to complete the Mental Health Map Inventory, a personalized tool that will help you track your progress and grow in key areas of mental health.

Thank you for engaging with this book! I hope it's been a supportive resource, helping you feel understood and empowered to thrive as your authentic self.

REFERENCES

Alba, B., A. Lyons, A. Waling, V. Minichiello, M. Hughes, C. Barrett, et al. 2020. "Older Lesbian and Gay Adults' Perceptions of Barriers and Facilitators to Accessing Health and Aged Care Services in Australia." *Health and Social Care in the Community* 29: 918–927.

Amato, A. T., and G. Émond. 2023. "A Systematic Review of Psychosocial Challenges for MSM Living with HIV Among Diverse and Intersecting Minorities." *The Canadian Journal of Human Sexuality* 32: 340–354.

Ayala, G., and A. Spieldenner. 2021. "HIV Is a Story First Written on the Bodies of Gay and Bisexual Men." *American Journal of Public Health* 111: 1240–1242.

Barrett-Ibarria, Sofia. 2018. "Queer Women Are Better at Breakups." *VICE*, May 16. https://www.vice.com/en/article/queer-women-are-better-at-breakups.

Barasz, K., and S. F. Hagerty. 2021. "Hoping for the Worst? A Paradoxical Preference for Bad News." *Journal of Consumer Research* 48: 270–288.

Batchelder, A. W., C. Fitch, B. A. Feinstein, A. Thiim, and C. O'Cleirigh. 2021. "Psychiatric, Substance Use, and Structural Disparities Between Gay and Bisexual Men with Histories of Childhood Sexual Abuse and Recent Sexual Risk Behavior." *Archives of Sexual Behavior* 50: 2861–2873.

Batista, I. C., and H. Pereira. 2020. "Mental Health, Resilience and HIV in Older Gay and Bisexual Men." *Educational Gerontology* 46: 525–539.

Blair, K. 2021. "Are LGBTQ+ People More Likely to Stay Friends with Their Exes?" *Psychology Today*, September 19. https://www.psychologytoday.com/us/blog/inclusive-insight/202109/are-lgbtq-people-more-likely-stay-friends-their-exes.

Bolton, J. 2009. "What We Get Wrong About Shame." *Psychology Today*, May 18. https://www.psychologytoday.com/za/blog/your-zesty-self/200905/what-we-get-wrong-about-shame.

Brown, B. 2013. "Shame vs. Guilt," Brené Brown, January 15. https://brenebrown.com/articles/2013/01/15/shame-v-guilt/.

Card, K. G., T. A. Hart, J. Flores Aranda, R. Ortiz Nunez, N. J. Lachowsky, T. Salway, and J. Jollimore. 2024. "Improving Substance Use Related Policies for Gay, Bisexual, and Queer Men." *Community-Based Research Centre*, May 21. https://www.cbrc.net/improving_substance_use_related_policies_for_gay_bisexual_and_queer_men.

Centre for Addiction and Mental Health. 2018. "Addiction." https://www.camh.ca/en/health-info/mental-illness-and-addiction-index/addiction.

Chabris, C., and D. Simons. 2011. *The Invisible Gorilla: How Our Intuitions Deceive Us*. New York: Broadway Paperbacks.

Cheung, W. Y., C. Sedikides, and T. Wildschut. 2017. "Nostalgia Proneness and Reduced Prejudice." *Personality and Individual Differences* 109: 89–97.

Cheves, Alexander. 2022. "Turning 30: What It Means When You're Gay." *Out*, May 10. https://www.out.com/print/2022/5/10/turning-30-when-it-means-when-youre-gay.

Cloud, J. 2008. "Are Gay Relationships Different?" *Time*, January 17. https://time.com/archive/6683459/are-gay-relationships-different.

Doka, K. J. 2008. "Disenfranchised Grief in Historical and Cultural Perspective." In *Handbook of Bereavement Research and Practice: Advances in Theory and Intervention*, edited by M. S. Stroebe, R. O. Hansson, H. Schut, and W. Stroebe. Washington, DC: American Psychological Association.

Dutcher, J. M., J. Lederman, M. Jain, S. Price, A. Kumar, D. K. Villalba, et al. 2022. "Lack of Belonging Predicts Depressive Symptomatology in College Students." *Psychological Science* 33: 1048–1067.

Eaton, L. A., A. Allen, J. L. Maksut, V. Earnshaw, R. J. Watson, & S. C. Kalichman. 2020. "HIV Microaggressions: A Novel Measure of Stigma-Related Experiences Among People Living with HIV." *Journal of Behavioral Medicine* 43: 34–43.

Epstein, J. 1992. "AIDS, Stigma, and Narratives of Containment." *American Imago* 49: 293–310.

Fredrick, E. G. 2017. "Development and Validation of the Bisexual Microaggressions Scale." PhD diss., East Tennessee State University. https://dc.etsu.edu/cgi/viewcontent.cgi?article=4735&context=etd.

Freedman, G., D. N. Powell, B. Le, and K. D. Williams. 2019. "Ghosting and Destiny: Implicit Theories of Relationships Predict Beliefs About Ghosting." *Journal of Social and Personal Relationships* 36: 905–924.

García-Gómez, A. 2024. "Examining Gay Male Discursive Practices in Hookup Apps: A Study on Mediated Intimacies and Aggressive Sexual Behaviours." *Journal of Language and Sexuality* 13: 154–177.

Gebru, N. M., S. S. Canidate, Y. Liu, S. E. Schaefer, E. Pavila, R. L. Cook, and R. F. Leeman. 2023. "Substance Use and Adherence to HIV Pre-Exposure Prophylaxis in Studies Enrolling Men Who Have Sex with Men and Transgender Women: A Systematic Review." *AIDS and Behavior* 27: 2131–2162.

Gibbs, J. J., and A. Baldwin-White. 2022. "Sexual Assault and Behavioral Health: What Can We Learn from a Probability Sample of Young Sexual Minority Men?" *Journal of Interpersonal Violence* 38: 2614–2629.

Gilbert, S. P., and S. K. Sifers. 2011. "Bouncing Back from a Breakup: Attachment, Time Perspective, Mental Health, and Romantic Loss." *Journal of College Student Psychotherapy* 25: 295–310.

Goldfarb, A. 2017. "Being Rejected Sucks, Here's How to Cope." VICE, July 18. https://www.vice.com/en/article/how-to-handle-rejection&/#8203.

Haines, M., P. O'Byrne, and P. MacPherson. 2021. "Gay, Bisexual, and Other Men Who Have Sex with Men: Barriers and Facilitators to Healthcare Access in Ottawa." *The Canadian Journal of Human Sexuality* 30: 339–348.

Hale, C. J., J. W. Hannum, and D. L. Espelage. 2005. "Social Support and Physical Health: The Importance of Belonging." *Journal of American College Health* 53: 276–284.

Hequembourg, A. L., K. A. Parks, R. L. Collins, and T. L. Hughes. 2014. "Sexual Assault Risks Among Gay and Bisexual Men." *The Journal of Sex Research* 52: 282–295.

Herie, M., L. Watkin-Merek, H. Annis, and Centre for Addiction and Mental Health. 2006. *Structured Relapse Prevention: An Outpatient Counselling Approach*. 2nd ed. Centre for Addiction and Mental Health.

Hickey, P. M., L. A. Best, and D. Speed. 2023. "Access to Healthcare and Unmet Needs in the Canadian Lesbian-Gay-Bisexual Population." *Journal of Homosexuality*: 1–19.

Hindes, S., and B. Fileborn. 2020. "Reporting on Sexual Violence 'Inside the Closet': Masculinity, Homosexuality and #MeToo." *Crime, Media, Culture: An International Journal* 17: 163–184.

Íncera-Fernández, D., M. Gámez-Guadix, and S. Moreno-Guillén. 2021. "Mental Health Symptoms Associated with Sexualized Drug Use (Chemsex) Among Men Who Have Sex with Men: A Systematic Review." *International Journal of Environmental Research and Public Health* 18: 13299.

Jaspal, R. 2015. "The Experience of Relationship Dissolution Among British South Asian Gay Men: Identity Threat and Protection." *Sexuality Research and Social Policy* 12: 34–46.

Johns, D. 2020. "We Need to Move Beyond Coming Out and Begin Inviting In." *The Advocate*, October 11. https://www.advocate.com/commentary/2020/10/11/we-need-move-beyond-coming-out-and-begin-inviting.

Johnson, T. R. 2023. "I Grappled with Masculinity. My Mother Showed Me the Truth." *The Washington Post*, May 9. https://www.washingtonpost.com/opinions/2023/05/09/grief-black-masculinity/.

Julian, J. M., J. I. Held, K. Hixson, and B. M. Conn. 2023. "The Implementation of Narrative Exposure Therapy (NET) for Transgender and Gender Diverse Adolescents and Young Adults." *Journal of Child and Adolescent Trauma* 16: 795–804.

Kleinhans, A. V. 2019. "Lesbian, Gay, Bisexual, Transgender, and Intersex (LGBTI) Students Are Scrambling for Access to Healthcare Services in the Campus Healthcare System: Perceptions of Key Informants." *South African Journal of Higher Education* 33: 213–229.

Koziol, Michael. 2015. "'Gay Death': They Say 30 Is the New 25." *The Sydney Morning Herald*, August 20. https://www.smh.com.au/opinion/gay-death-they-say-30-new-25-20150819-gj3726.html.

Krouse, L. 2023. "If You're Mourning Lost Time Right Now, You're Not the Only One." Self, February 23. https://www.self.com/story/grieving-lost-time.

LeFebvre, L. E., M. Allen, R. D. Rasner, S. Garstad, A. Wilms, and C. Parrish. 2019. "Ghosting in Emerging Adults' Romantic Relationships: The Digital Dissolution Disappearance Strategy." *Imagination, Cognition and Personality* 39: 125–150.

Levy, B. 2022. *Breaking the Age Code: How Your Beliefs About Aging Determine How Long and Well You Live*. New York: William Morrow.

Maslow, A. H. 1943. "A Theory of Human Motivation." *Psychological Review* 50: 370–396.

McCann, E., M. J. Brown, and J. Taylor. 2020. "The Views and Experiences of Bisexual People Regarding Their Psychosocial Support Needs: A Qualitative Evidence Synthesis." *Journal of Psychiatric and Mental Health Nursing* 28: 430–443.

McGuire, M., K. G. Card, K. Fulcher, G. Berlin, A. Wells, T. Nguyen, and N. J. Lachowsky. 2020. "The Crystal Methamphetamine Project: Understanding the Need for Culturally-Safe Supports and Services Addressing Crystal Methamphetamine Use Among Gay, Bi, and Queer Men." *Canadian Institute for Substance Use Research.*

Medina, C., and L. Mahowald. 2023. "Discrimination and Barriers to Well-Being: The State of the LGBTQI+ Community in 2022." Center for American Progress, January 12. https://www.americanprogress.org/article/discrimination-and-barriers-to-well-being-the-state-of-the-lgbtqi-community-in-2022/.

Moeller, R. W., M. Seehuus, and V. Peisch. 2020. "Emotional Intelligence, Belongingness, and Mental Health in College Students." *Frontiers in Psychology* 11.

Moon, S. S., V. L. Timbers, S. C. Boddie, S. R. Ryan-Pettes, and L. Anderson. 2024. "Multiple Risk Factors of Substance Use Among Lesbian, Gay, Bisexual (LGB) Adults: A Comparison Study." *Journal of Human Behavior in the Social Environment* 34: 926–937.

Nadal, K. L., A. Skolnik, and Y. Wong. 2012. "Interpersonal and Systemic Microaggressions Toward Transgender People: Implications for Counseling." *Journal of LGBT Issues in Counseling* 6: 55–82.

Nathanson, Donald. 1997. "Affect Theory and the Compass of Shame." In *The Widening Scope of Shame*, edited by Melvin R. Lansky and Andrew P. Morrison. New York: Psychology Press: 339–354.

Navarro, R., E. Larrañaga, S. Yubero, and B. Víllora. 2020a. "Ghosting and Breadcrumbing: Prevalence and Relations with Online Dating Behaviors Among Young Adults." *Escritos De Psicología* 13: 46–59.

Navarro, R., E. Larrañaga, S. Yubero, and B. Víllora. 2020b. "Psychological Correlates of Ghosting and Breadcrumbing Experiences: A Preliminary Study Among Adults." *International Journal of Environmental Research and Public Health* 17: 1116.

Oakley, L. 2020. "Breakups Are Hard — But for Bi People They Can Be Life-Changing." *Bi.org*, July 28. https://bi.org/en/articles/breakups-can-be-hard-but-they-also-create-opportunity.

Paradis, C., Butt, P., Shield, K., Poole, N., Wells, S., Naimi, T., et al. 2023. *Canada's Guidance on Alcohol and Health: Final Report*. Ottawa, Ont.: Canadian Centre on Substance Use and Addiction.

Paul, M. 2011. "Why We Feel Shame and How to Conquer It," The Blog, *HuffPost*, updated December 6. https://www.huffpost.com/entry/dealing-with-shame_b_994991.

Pearlman, L. A., C. B. Wortman, C. A. Feuer, C. H. Farber, and T. A. Rando. 2014. *Treating Traumatic Bereavement: A Practitioner's Guide*. New York: Guilford Press.

Peterson, M., K. Nowotny, E. Dauria, T. Arnold, and L. Brinkley-Rubinstein. 2018. "Institutional Distrust Among Gay, Bisexual, and Other Men Who Have Sex with Men as a Barrier to Accessing Pre-exposure Prophylaxis (PrEP)." *AIDS Care* 31: 364–369.

Pierce, C. 1970. "Offensive Mechanisms." In *The Black Seventies*, edited by F. B. Barbour. Boston: Porter Sargent.

Rakshit, D. 2023. "The Link Between Neurodivergence and Queerness, Explained." *THE SWDL*, April 28. https://www.theswaddle.com/why-theres-more-gender-and-sexuality-diversity-in-the-neurodivergent-community.

Rosenfeld, D. 2018. "The AIDS Epidemic's Lasting Impact on Gay Men." Blog, The British Academy, February 19. https://www.thebritishacademy.ac.uk/blog/aids-epidemic-lasting-impact-gay-men/.

Salehuddin, A. S., T. D. Afifi, and J. Salmon. 2024. "Conscious Uncoupling: Divorce in the 21st Century." In *Modern Relationships: Romance, Friendship, and Family in the 21st Century*, edited by M. Hojjat and A. Moyer. Oxford: Oxford University Press, 141–157.

Salter, M., K. Robinson, J. Ullman, N. Denson, G. Ovenden, K. Noonan, et al. 2020. "Gay, Bisexual, and Queer Men's Attitudes and Understandings of Intimate Partner Violence and Sexual Assault." *Journal of Interpersonal Violence* 36: 11630–11657.

Sanchez, A. A. 2017. "The Whiteness of 'Coming Out': Culture and Identity in the Disclosure Narrative." *Archer Magazine*, July 7. https://archermagazine.com.au/2017/07/culture-coming-out/.

Saunders, R. K., D. C. Carr, and A. M. Burdette. 2023. "Health Care Stereotype Threat and Sexual and Gender Minority Well-Being." *Journal of Health and Social Behavior* 65: 20–37.

Scherrer, R., and M. Dinman. 2023. "Internalized Ageism – Discriminating Against Ourselves as We Age." Harvey A. Friedman Center for Aging, Institute for Public Health, March 28. https://publichealth.wustl.edu/internalized-ageism-discriminating-against-ourselves-as-we-age.

Sell, R., and E. Krims. 2021. "Structural Transphobia, Homophobia, and Biphobia in Public Health Practice: The Example of COVID-19 Surveillance." *American Journal of Public Health*: 111.

Spendelow, J. 2020. "Healthy Grieving in Men Through Flexible Masculinity." Psychology Today, March 23. https://www.psychologytoday.com/us/blog/bravery-in-bereavement/202003/healthy-grieving-in-men-through-flexible-masculinity.

Sternin, S., R. M. McKie, C. Winberg, R. N. Travers, T. P. Humphreys, and E. D. Reissing. 2021. "Sexual Consent: Exploring the Perceptions of Heterosexual and Non-Heterosexual Men." *Psychology and Sexuality* 13: 512–534.

Thawer, R. 2022. "Sexuality and the Imprint of Shame: What Queer Guys (and Their Therapists) Need to Know — Part 1/3." *Medium*, January 19. https://medium.com/@rahimthawer/sexuality-and-the-imprint-of-shame-what-queer-guys-and-their-therapists-need-to-know-part-1-3-4e5bd7caeca7.

Zhou, X., C. Sedikides, T. Wildschut, and D. G. Gao. 2008. "Counteracting Loneliness: On the Restorative Function of Nostalgia." *Psychological Science* 19: 1023–1029.

Rahim Thawer, MSW, RSW, is a clinical social worker and psychotherapist from Toronto, ON, Canada. He is a clinical supervisor, facilitator and public speaker, university instructor, writer, and host of *The CBT Dive* podcast. He's trained in cognitive behavioral therapy (CBT), Gestalt, psychoanalytic, and sex therapy approaches. His clinical practice and writing explore the intersection of systemic oppression and mental health, while also honoring innovation in queer relationships.

Foreword writer **Leo Herrera** is a queer Mexican artist who explores queer and immigrant experiences through the lenses of sex, technology, and history. His work centers on themes of disease and stigma, always searching for utopia in LGBTQ history's darkest chapters. Herrera is director of *Fathers*, a multimedia project which imagines the world if AIDS never existed. He is author of *Analog Cruising*, a manual for modern sex outside of our phones.

Real change *is* possible

For more than fifty years, New Harbinger has published proven-effective self-help books and pioneering workbooks to help readers of all ages and backgrounds improve mental health and well-being, and achieve lasting personal growth. In addition, our spirituality books offer profound guidance for deepening awareness and cultivating healing, self-discovery, and fulfillment.

Founded by psychologist Matthew McKay and Patrick Fanning, New Harbinger is proud to be an independent, employee-owned company. Our books reflect our core values of integrity, innovation, commitment, sustainability, compassion, and trust. Written by leaders in the field and recommended by therapists worldwide, New Harbinger books are practical, accessible, and provide real tools for real change.

MORE BOOKS from
NEW HARBINGER PUBLICATIONS

THE QUEER AND TRANSGENDER RESILIENCE WORKBOOK
Skills for Navigating Sexual Orientation and Gender Expression
978-1626259461 / US $25.95

ALL PARTS WELCOME
The Queer and Trans Internal Family Systems Workbook
978-1648485282 / US $24.95

I'M NOT OKAY AND THAT'S OKAY
Mental Health Microskills to Deal with Life's Inevitable Struggles
978-1648481758 / US $18.95

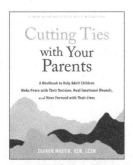

CUTTING TIES WITH YOUR PARENTS
A Workbook to Help Adult Children Make Peace with Their Decision, Heal Emotional Wounds, and Move Forward with Their Lives
978-1648483905 / US $25.95

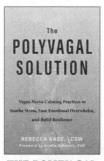

THE POLYVAGAL SOLUTION
Vagus Nerve-Calming Practices to Soothe Stress, Ease Emotional Overwhelm, and Build Resilience
978-1648484124 / US $19.95

THE SELF-COMPASSION DAILY JOURNAL
Let Go of Your Inner Critic and Embrace Who You Are with Acceptance and Commitment Therapy
978-1648482496 / US $18.95

newharbingerpublications
1-800-748-6273 / newharbinger.com

(VISA, MC, AMEX / prices subject to change without notice)
Follow Us

Don't miss out on new books from New Harbinger.
Subscribe to our email list at **newharbinger.com/subscribe**

Did you know there are **free tools** you can download for this book?

Free tools are things like **worksheets**, **guided meditation exercises**, and **more** that will help you get the most out of your book.

You can download free tools for this book—whether you bought or borrowed it, in any format, from any source—from the New Harbinger website. All you need is a NewHarbinger.com account. Just use the URL provided in this book to view the free tools that are available for it. Then, click on the "download" button for the free tool you want, and follow the prompts that appear to log in to your NewHarbinger.com account and download the material.

You can also save the free tools for this book to your **Free Tools Library** so you can access them again anytime, just by logging in to your account! Just look for this button on the book's free tools page.

+ Save this to my free tools library

If you need help accessing or downloading free tools, visit **newharbinger.com/faq** or contact us at **customerservice@newharbinger.com**.